The Girlfriend's List

by
Izola Bird

I0118366

Published by

DoriNu Publications, LLC
Dayton, OH
DorindaDENusum.com

Published by **DORINU PUBLICATIONS, LLC**

DoriNu Publications, LLC
Dayton, OH
DorindaDENusum.com

This book is a work of fiction. Names, characters, places, and incidents are products of the authors' imagination and are used fictitiously. Any resemblance to actual events, locales, or persons, living or dead, is entirely coincidental.

This ideas in this book do not reflect the views or opinions of DoriNu Publications.

ISBN-13: 978-0-9835662-5-0

Printed in the United States of America

Introduction

After venting in my first book, *The Witch Who Stole My Husband*, which I wrote in 2010, I thought I would write something more calming that everyone could enjoy - the young, the young at heart, and simply to those who want to remember. Mostly, I've written this new book for young women and young men. It's about listing things that usually proceed in love. The book is hopefully humorous with a reality mix to calm one's nerves while reading it.

I must admit when I begin to write a book, I always do a little research. I looked at tons of movies and read lots of books for this one. I had already written this book, but put it in my piles of piles and it gathered dust throughout the years along with my countless numbers of short stories.

It wasn't until I was watching the Oprah Show one day, when a guy was talking about his book; *He's Not That Into You,* the brainchild of writer Greg Behrendt. That brainchild could have been mine!

As Behrendt sat there explaining to Oprah how he came up with the idea, I ran to my piles of piles and dusted off my book entitled, *The Girl Friend's List.* I thought, "Here is my chance - that big moment that every writer waits for."

You see, I had the master plan all along somewhere stacked up in my basement. I had become so fearful that publishers would reject it as they have done with my work in the past. I didn't want to go through another day feeling sorry for myself and thinking about those stupid publishers who could have otherwise had a bestseller on their hands.

If it weren't for self-publishing and small publishers, I would have never beaten the odds of getting my books out there.

As time went on, I had a lot of short stories and articles published and I am grateful for that, but we all want something more.

Friends on my Face Book page told me to stop relying on the publisher and do it myself. That would cost too much money, I thought, and then I would have to find ways of marketing and promoting my own books.

I thrived on the traditional way, but my name was very small in the sea of authors, so I tried a different approach. I've collected piles of rejection letters throughout the years. In fact I need to publish all rejection letters I've received along with the envelopes.

There was another book I had to take a look at while doing my research and reviews on the books. It's called, *Why Hasn't He Called Me?* This book is a good book for women to read. I say that because a man wrote it, so it gives the female reader some idea as to how men think or were thinking at the time. Since my books are mostly
about the wrongs men do, these books are useful tools for me.

Steve Harvey's book, *Act Like A Lady And Think Like A Man* is another good book. When I first heard the title, I thought, what a bunch of nonsense, but after reading the book, I became jealous and judgmental.

When they write from a woman's point of view, do these male authors stop to think about what their mothers were going through? Steve Harvey

—

seems to praise his father for being a womanizer, and how he developed his player's card through him. Was I right? Well, this is what I was thinking.

As I read on I felt he was laughing at us for being so ignorant of men and why they cheat. Sex doesn't keep a man at home and feeding him an excellent meal won't either. I said to myself, "He needs to read my book, The Witch Who Stole My Husband, and then he'll change his tune." Through it all though, I really liked Steve Harvey's book.

I met another guy along the way when I was at one of my book signings in Houston, Texas. The guy had self-published a book called, "Cheat to Keep Your Marriage." Rather than debating with the guy at the table next to me, we exchanged books. He kept trying to tell me it's a woman's fault when men cheat. I didn't want to hear that. It was a human's foolish error to think they could keep making up excuses as to why they committed adultery and fell alright about getting away with it. Just like in any relationship, we have choices.

I'm not trying to give a shout out or plug to the movies I watched, but after reaching my own conclusion, I found out they all had something in common, with the book I was writing, "The Girlfriend's List."

I watched and took notes on movies *Hitch, Breaking all the Rules, The List* with Wayne Brady and Sidney Poitier daughter, who's named after her legendary father, *7 Things To Do Before I'm 30, Double Wedding* with Tia and Tamara Mowry, *Sleepless in Seattle, Eat Pray, Love,* (which by the way was a very good movie with Julia Roberts), The movie *Dance with Me* with Vanessa Williams and the handsome

Chayanne. Okay, so I've given shout-outs to the movies.

Shame on those snobbish, nosey, Hollywood people who make a living by distorting the truth. From the critic corner, I give the thumbs down on some of those stupid movies the critics picked as good. They need to talk to some of us regular folks who really know what needs to be written in order to create romantic movies and stories about comedic relationships.

I would catch some movies on the Hallmark Channel, which I call "the good girl" channel that I could simply enjoy with no outrageous, wild sex. It doesn't sound fun, but I just wanted to see what they were all about and I did.

Throughout this book, at times, so that I capture the attention of people of all age groups for whom this information applies, I am going to begin writing in the language of everyone today, including those that use text messaging, so you just might see words like ur 2 cute 2 b true written in here.

This book was really fun 2 do especially after reading Dana Dorfman's, A Woman's Intuition on-line. I had to find the book. What can I say? I like to read everything I can get my hands on while I'm researching material for my books. I have read some books that my friends won't even dare to read because they think it will distort their beliefs on some kind of religious standing. I did read a lot and watched a lot, and I hope my research proves worthy in providing you with a good book. Enjoy!

In the following pages, beware:

***

THERE ARE NO MISSPELLED WORDS JUST YOUR BRAINS ON TEXT MESSAGING! 4 U OLDER GENERATIONS, I STUCK TO MOST OF THE QUEEN'S ENGLISH. I didn't add a lot of ur, (your) nvrmd (never mind) r, (are) u (you) cm (come) luv (love) Lol (laughing out loud) stuff like that! I just put enough to drive you a little crazy, that's all! ☺

Table of Contents

CHAPTER 1
Boy Meets Girl

As I sat there interviewing an older man a younger guy who looked to be in his early thirties was eager to jump in on our conversation. The older man was giving me something straight from his experience about younger people. You might just think, "well, he's older, so all older people tend to think this way." Here's to the older man's opinion:

"It seems all young people want to do is dance, party and entertain themselves and shy away from deep women-men commitments. They will have children whether they are committed or not. They will see each other 8 to 9 times a months and the girl will end up getting pregnant. "It's not mine," the guy will say each time. That guy would probably have been me if I were the one insisting that she should have been on some kind of birth control and if I wasn't using condoms. I never wanted kids outside of marriage. I always asked, "R u using protection?" and even if she said she was, I was still packing. Sometimes I would be so bold as to ask to see what she was using.

I would go as far as looking at her birth control container to see what day she was
on," the older man said.

The eager younger man couldn't wait until the man finished his input and offered me his thoughts right before I was able to ask my next question.

"Pardon me, ma'am," he smiled.

"Ma'am," I said politely, but with a stern tone to my voice. My own kids aren't allowed to call me ma'am. Do you know where ma'am originated from?" I asked him.

"No, ma' am," he said clearing his throat as if he made a huge mistake again.

I don't want to tell u everything that I said to him just yet, because I would be interrupting what I need to finish telling you about my story, so in order to find out later, you will have to wait until you read on. If u just can't wait, find the page titled, "Pardon me Ma'am."

The younger man wanted to join in on our conversation with a few questions of his own first before telling me what was on his mind. I ended up telling him I was writing a book. I looked up at his tall frame and gentle smile and asked him to have a seat. Boom, he flat out and said it again! "Ma'am". If I were a ma'am don't u think he would have just shown me some kind of respect? Maybe he was just using ma'am as an excuse like we all do 2 b polite, the way we were trained 2 be at some point in our lives. Either way, I didn't like the word, "Ma'am."

Anyhow, the younger man told me, "We don't like using condoms, because it doesn't feel right. My first time having sex was natural, and the girl said she was on birth control and I believed her. When time passed, she told me she wasn't, and I was upset, because I could have gotten her pregnant.

It was my first time and apparently hers as well. Now, I do use condoms and I do ask if the girl is using protection. This experience scared me so bad I quickly got used to the feel of them. Now, they've got all kinds that feel natural. For me, it's all about experiencing the natural feeling of a woman inside, but I advise all young people not to do it carelessly, because they might risk having a bad experience.

The same diseases are out there, no matter how they change the name. Man, I was reading this book that said AIDS was out during the 1970's and maybe before.

The other bad experience is that guys might just get a girl pregnant. Girls these days don't care, because they don't want us to use condoms. I'm thirty-three years old, and one girl I dated was 28 years old. She told me not to use a condom. I said to myself, "She must be out of her mind!" All I could see was a baby and that's something I don't want! I see what my brother is going through....no I don't want to be that guy.

The Tarzan Meet Jane Syndrome

When Tarzan met Jane, he couldn't understand a word she said and she couldn't understand him. They understood one thing about each other and that was physical attraction. He liked her and she liked him. They exchanged glances and smiled and teasing one another until finally, Tarzan got up the nerve to introduce himself. Tarzan's heart started beating faster as he approached Jane. Jane felt weak in the knees. Even though she couldn't understand a word he said, it didn't matter because he was so cute.

"I'm Tarzan U Jane," says Tarzan.

"That's cool," you want to have sex.

The ritual begins:

"Come on, Jane. Let's dance"

"Okay, Tarzan I feel romance!"

That is how it goes today. Girls don't even get a last name. They just want to swing from some boy's tree without getting to know him first. Then, one day Tarzan discovers you have moved in and he can't do what he wants to do in his man cave. (The word man cave was banned; because they said some women who were always sticking their noses in the man caves overrated it. I like this saying, but it will fade too just like a lot of other colorful metaphors...but for now, the people have spoken...who ever they r.)

He's tired of Jane, and she has to go! He didn't know it was going to be so much trouble. He comes home one day, there's a flower on the coconut table, and he has a closet filled with shirts and pants. After going without a shirt just fine, now, he has to watch his manners and put on a nice shirt when he goes outside. This makes him what to holler. That's why he goes outside his used-to-be man cave and does it.

You know that famous holler he had that was so sexy in the beginning when you met him? Now, he uses it because he has no space. He feels trapped.

The second day he comes home your beautiful shape is changing. He's wondering what's wrong. You are crying.

"Jane, what's bothering u?" Tarzan asks.

"What do u think? I'm pregnant!" she yells. Tarzan starts speaking in that language that he was speaking when he first met Jane. Jane can't understand a word he says. He can't understand her either! Well, not until she starts talking in the universal language, Child Support!

Because of all the mama drama she will soon dish out, her chance of ever getting that big rock on her finger will lessen.

Why can't dogs and cats get along?
Cats like 2 purr and dogs like 2 roam!

Chapter 2

The male thing:

The first definition of a man: A man is a visual creature. They are a walking pair of legs, handsomely created, muscles, loaded with testosterone, and equipped with x-ray vision. I'm talking about your man! Your girlfriend's man and your daddy too!

You don't have to get it through ur head that a male is a visual creature, because they will teach you this lesson throughout life. Yeah, *creature* deriving from the word create-creation-creature anything created. His gorgeous green eyes, or soft chestnut brown if you prefer, sees only the heavenly body of Venus. That's u or your mom! Mostly u!

What a guy sees?

Nvrmnd what you think. Just toss it out. He sees a Venus with boobs and legs walking towards him with the most awesome heavenly body. Nvrmnd a man to answer honestly, this is what he might say.

"I rather respect your body first and then ur mind last."

Example:

I was walking out of a particular place at a particular time. There was this gorgeous blonde girl in front of me walking as if she were in a hurry. I felt a breeze rush pass me as if I were trapped inside a commercial. Her silky, luxurious hair was swinging from side to side and she had on short shorts with a nice top that showed off her figure even more. She had an hourglass shape and nice long legs.

A young man had passed the both of us before she stepped out of the automatic glass doors. It seems at that moment a clean cut, average looking, tall guy beat her to the manual doors from the automatic glass doors and held it open 4 her. If it weren't for me quickly moving my foot out of the way I could have suffered some serious injuries.

My body made it half-way thorough the manual doors leading to outside the building from closing on my foot. I was smiling about the fact that his reaction was all but caring about my foot. He wasn't paying any attention to me as he was offering the flirtiest comments to her outside. He wasn't aware that I was a part of this involuntarily scene. I saw him smiling and walking backwards just to keep the conversation going as she tossed her bouncy hair with her right hand. It seemed as if it were a normal thing for her to do, and yes she did it well. Her hair hit the air in slow motion in the breeze that was coming in.

The guy had stopped to watch her as he took his phone out of his pocket to call one of his friends"She's hot," he said. His words, not mine. In my own movie, which played in my mind, she was what some would consider a picture-perfect magazine cover girl. This wasn't happening in Hollywood, but on the streets of downtown some where in Indiana. Before she turns the corner, four other men couldn't keep their eyes off her either. Then, I thought if I had I been a little younger (okay, okay, a lot younger) he would have kept that door open for me. If I were fat and out of shape with my belly hanging to my knees my poor foot would have been hurt.

I thought at least the door stayed open wide enough to get my 5-foot frame half way through keeping the door from injuring my foot. Then, I thought, it probably didn't have anything 2 do with my age, but simply the woman looking like she just stepped out off the cover of a magazine. Maybe it just had something 2 do with him being a man.

In this unfortunate moment, we both were headed in the same direction of the parking lot. In my mind, I could see myself walking up to him and politely telling him he almost slammed the door on my foot. I thought about so many things, but none of them were the right thing to do, so I didn't walk up to him. The young woman was still on his mind and in his voice as he talked on the phone to a friend about her.

I saw him get in his car and take off. Unfortunately, for me, the opportunity presented itself as he couldn't get out of the gate. He had left and forgotten to get the code off the guard's desk.

While he was flirting, I wrote down the number. He couldn't get outside the gate and my car was right behind his. He waved his hand telling me to back up. I waved the paper to him and yelled out of my car, "I got the code!" He smiled and got out of his car to get the number. I laughed, and yes, that was the right opportunity. I said with laughter in my voice, "You were too busy flirting with that girl...ha...ahaa..you forgot the number." He laughed and returned an honesty answer, "You're right."

I never mentioned the fact that he almost slammed the door on my foot in the mist of his flirting. I'm such a romantic; I had the nerve to even think it was cute.

The day after the guy almost hit my foot in the door. I was talking to another young man about 38 years old. While he was talking I'm thinking that shouldn't u b thinking about marriage or something. He was eagerly, to tell me his story, but his phone ringing, and I gather from that point he want me to listen as well. I'm writing a book, well, yeah, and I needed his imput! From the sound of his conversation he had been talking to his friend before.

"The girl couldn't handle the break up. My ex girlfriend exploded when we broke up. The girl came over my house and I moved back in with my parents so I could go back to (college) school. We heard a window break outside. We I looked out the window, dude, she broke out my car window. I had to call the police on her. I didn't even call her mom, and I luv her mother. She's crazy! At first she was handling it well. She really couldn't handle it. We just couldn't get along any more. The next thing I knew, a couple of days later, she exploded!"
He looked at me, and tapped me on the shoulder, they say we can't handle break-ups.

The Second Definition of a Man:

He used 2 b respected for his mind, not the size of his wallet. Men were once considered great thinkers, scientists, inventors, artists, poets, and great writers. Now, men are respect by who says he's the sexiest man of the year. Who ever came up with this dumb idea? No wonder he can't create or invent like he used 2 (with some exceptions).

Pull a man out of a sewer who's been working all day and night with dirt and sweat running down his brown muscles that won't quit...Now, that's sexy.

Some men are pleased to c u happy. Some women aren't pleased 2 c u pleased.

The Man Thing - He Who Conquers

The Third Definition:

Deep thinkers, sit, scratch, spit, curse, drink, rules, protect their beer, beer can crushers, scary drivers, sport crazed, secretive, remote holders, handsomely made, problem solvers, passes gas and think it's funny, cries when he's deeply hurt such as death and breaking up with someone he really loves, fighting over custody of his children and marriage, but yet showing himself as a lion in it all.

Loves his man cave and don't want u in it. Loves his man movies, even the kinds we don't want to mention. He really doesn't want to watch our lovesick movies. Sometimes he tolerates them to keep us quiet. His mind is really somewhere else. Notice this is why he falls asleep or can't wait until his friends call.

The tool he has between his legs makes him think he is a god or at least somebody's god when he is making love. Women are supposed to be lucky that they are in his presence. His ego is like a high ejaculation. He has line-a-sight is really his emotional make up. If he can see u naked it turns him on far better than tight jeans and spiked heels.

He can be caring and loving in all of his madness. He likes to remain in control. He doesn't want to be a ready-made father, but becomes a willing sort if he's in love with you. He's never ready for parenthood, especially when he is not asked or doing the asking. He will say he'll only love you, but will love and make love to many.

He's a conqueror that loses his hair early, and has to prove that he's a man, baby. Mid-life crisis doesn't sit well with him, and he sees it as an opportunity to sow his wild oats. When this happens, he is in the mood for love, because he has a problem to solve, which in returns loose his scent - testosterone.

When his testosterone mostly remains high, so he can have the POWER! He will never admit when it is low and won't see a doctor if you suggest he does. He thanks God for the little blue pill, especially if he's older. When his testosterone is high he's at his most romantic, energetic, strong, and passionate self! It's like he's superman on steroids. POWERFUL!

But when all is said and done, when a man loves a woman u have all of him and nothing can separate the love he has 4 u. His conquest is to conquer not to be conquered. He is the chaser and doesn't like to be chased, and sure he'll go along with it just to get what he wants like sex. He is the leader and not to be lead. We should be thankful for being made of him and not him of us.

No matter how out of order the world seems to be men are still the masters of their domain. He is the natural born leader and no one can take his place. That's the order of things and that's how it will always be. So, for us girls, if u have a weak man, it's because society groomed him that way by making him feel inadequate and less than a man.

Then, we have the nerve to make him feel this way in his own home. Who's the man? Certainly not the woman (the gift), no matter how many female hormone injections and body transformation we go through.

A Little known fact:
A female responds to simulation
A male responds to penetration

CHAPTER 3
The Women Thing - We Will Never Conquer

Women accept the sitting, scratching, spitting, profanity, gas-passing, thinking it's funny, remote holding, and respect the security protectors. Man, no matter how terrible he is, a woman always hope he will change. They love the intimacy, lovemaking and yes, letting him think he's a god in bed even though he doesn't do a good job!

He is "The man." She doesn't want to bruise his ego, but she still hasn't learned that he connects with sight and not feely and emotional things. The woman is the feely emotional rollercoaster. *"Hell has no fury like woman scorned".* We often quote things wrong, but it was William Congreve in The Mourning Bride in 1697 that wrote this great piece (play) with those famous words. Why did he say it? What was really behind his words? This would be something good for us to look up.

She doesn't really understand the words, "letting go," because she can bring up things that happened five years ago when she's angry. She is wonderfully made and knows it, but doesn't weed out the fact that she doesn't always come with ribbons and bows in a pretty little box. She's not always "pretty in pink." Pink is just not her color any more and she can't even think of the last time she really liked it.

Guys, here is a hint just for u. Please move the hot grease and boiling water out of her way! Cupid doesn't live here any more, because the emotional roller coaster has begun.

She relies on her emotions, how she feels. She relies on her memory, what she heard and what happen yesterday and in the past. Her friends are like the Bible to her. When they tell her something, she really believes it. Unfortunately, we all make things to fix our own lives. R we reading it right! R we hearing it right! Or do we just want to b right!

If u don't know by now, she's nurturing and needs to feel needed, happy and loved, conversation walking magnet and if you haven't been drawn into her conversation, she will immediately think you are ignoring her or don't want to be bothered. There, I said a mouth full. At least pretend you are understanding by nodding your head and smiling a lot. It will help also if you notice anniversaries, birthdays, "the day we first met" around the corner at the coffee shop, out dancing, at a cheap restaurant or some where in time that you met your "dreamboat," - the luv of your life.

When these needs aren't met, she looses a powerful hormonal scent, oxytocin, "*the hormones of love*." (Dr. Grey) If you want to learn more about oxytocin, I do suggest you read other books on the matter. One of my favorites is written by Dr. Grey, *Men are from Mars and Women are from Venus.* For some of you older people, Venus is on Fire and Mars is on Ice. This will also help you grow old gracefully after 40. Hear that girls! Keeping a woman happy is the most important thing. Hear that guys!

One thing I will share that Dr. Grey said is, "Oxytocin is the hormone of love, while testosterone is the hormone of desire. When women are feeling happy and in love, their oxytocin level is high!" Hear that guys!

For you younger pups, you don't have to worry about all that stuff because your testosterone level is very high from a teenager to 30 years of age.

Its goes slightly goes down when you reach your thirties. Not to worry though because you still pack a whopper and can make sex good and exciting and that means more orgasms for your partner.

Take it like this: I just gave you something to look forward to in your old age. Hey, I don't think you're old, but you will when you get there, and everybody that's under you will make you feel old when you're still well in the prime of your life. The only thing that will interfere with your drive is over-abuse of alcohol and drugs. If you consume too much of these things, later in life you find that something is wrong with junior and you need a little help from your friendly doctor or over the counter friend.

You can read more about this juicy conversation when you read the chapter on Late Life Love Quotes from Connie Goldman.

I must tell you this: Another time when I was out renting movies, there was a tall dark and handsome guy that said to me, "My wife is in the mood for a walk in the park and hand holding. She wants movies that would reflect how she is feeling.

You know, romance. She wants to eat chocolate, and her favorite food - pasta. She wants to be fed chocolate covered strawberries and she likes to compare me with the guys in the movies." Then he said, "When they give u that list it's more to the list. Us guys get it all done, but then women want more. The list gets longer when she pops in the movie of her choice. I will accommodate her because it will make my life easier that day. She will expect me to watch these silly romance movies with her and her asking sounds more like a demand. If men were smart, they would play the role."

A woman is never meant 2 be conqueror just understood and that is hard for her 2 master. Guys can't understand the complexities of a woman, so men don't even try. Just go along with the program that was made 4 u. Oh yeah, and the chocolates, guys, is our stress reliever! Bring on the boxes of chocolate and forget the dieter's kind, because when we are in this kind of mood any kind of chocolate will do! (To read more about chocolate go to Delusion or Conclusion - Chocolate Bon-Bons)

A woman who never listens
is like a sunken ship
Even when she goes down she still doesn't know
When to be quiet or bridle her lips.

CHAPTER 4
Genetic seasoning 4 ur reasoning

Remember, the things in you came from your great great grandmother. The way we look a man and find him desirable.

True! Women from generation after generation have passed their knowledge on to us whether bad or good. If you can't remember them either giving you a list of things to do or running to the store (more commonly shopping centers) to get things for them it's okay.

Today, you might be in the home of a caregiver. Everybody starts out with a list. Every mother should want her son to turn out to be a good man. I will excuse the lost mothers - you know the ones who seems to be lost in space, the ones who got off the course of life due to no fault of their own. Or the one that just doesn't give a care! Hey, it could have happened to any one of us. Just when u thought you were the good one, life will teach u something new.

Men don't even realize that the list keeper is a part of a big plot. Plot seems to be a really weird word to use right? Have you looked up the meaning? It doesn't have to mean deceptive, but in some case it does.

Women use the list to their own advantage. It neither has to be for evil nor secrets. We don't mean to be dishonest, but sometimes it happens. I am going to define plot in the simplest way.

Sometimes, women use the plot for a particular purpose. In this purpose women go through a list of things we are made of. Before we even think about getting married it starts with the girlfriend's list. You see it's already been installed in the woman to give the list to the man.

How much I love Thee

On August 20-23 I was invited to CushCity for a book signing there I met a guy named Kevin Howard. He was among the group of authors who was invited for a book singing in Houston, Texas as well. Like most authors who participated in the event, we either exchanged information or exchanged books after the event ended. You never know where these things may lead, because sometimes authors don't keep in touch and I don't know the reason for it. For those who do, something good usually comes out of it.

After reading Kevin's book, I decided to contact him. The man was a master at writing love letters. I didn't know that he had it in him. I expressed that he should write a romance novel. I told him I was writing a book entitled, *The Girlfriend's List*. I wanted his opinion on the list. He

in return wrote me these things. "Women are fascinating because they think emotionally, whereas, men think practically. Not to say that women aren't practical. Napoleon Bonaparte is quoted as saying, "Men consider their needs, whereas women focus on their abilities." Being of the opposite sex and adoring women, I always look for their most endearing features. Like granddad would tell us as young boys. "Better a diamond with a flaw, than a pebble without." Putting that into context of having a woman to giving me a 'to-do' list, personally a list wouldn't bother me. (with the exception of picking up her feminine hygiene products). 'To-do' lists help with efficiency and productivity. From an aerospace perspective, a checklist is a good tool to utilize. At least I know where that is. Maybe it's a man aversion of having his woman giving him a list, as if he can't remember or isn't listening from the jump. (Or even worse, the aversion of having a woman telling him what to do!) However, a confident man wouldn't raise a question about why you are giving him a checklist. A confident man might make a joke about a checklist, but he wouldn't complain about it. That reminds me of a Groucho Marx joke, "Only one man in a1,000 is a leader of men. The other lower percentage follow women!" Of that is the case, a man's to-do/checklist should also contain what tickles her fancy. That reminds me of a lesson learned. 'Love is the delusion
that one woman is different from another.' Now where is that stupid list honey?"

That colorful paragraph of Kevin Howard's is very direct. I didn't change a thing. The man is a great writer. I read his book, *Letters to my Lover*, about the wonderful feeling of being in love. Some of his writing reminds me of the Songs of Solomon, true and with such great passion.

Kevin writes in his book: "Autumn, my mind's eye pictures our tie together at the wedding. The joy on your face and the smell of your essence still linger in my mind (page 32). Reading his letters to Autumn would bring every woman's heart to envy, and shame to have a man that doesn't write love letters.

A man who still writes love letter is worth any woman's time.

CHAPTER 5
Whoops, My Fault!

There was a woman that I knew who confused the list with intimacy. She had been just hanging out with a guy, and yes it resulted a month of "good sex." Well, those were her exact words. She was sure that she and this guy were a package deal.

Clearly, she didn't know the rules of dating, especially having sex and not getting to know the guy. For some of us slower people, we know a good night of sex doesn't turn into a relationship. For some of us who would rather marry than to burn, we follow the rule of never have sex first. Either they r 2 old fashioned or having a great sense of the old school way of doing things.

The woman went to the man's job (the one she was dating) and left a note on his car asking why he hadn't called her. (If it's beginning to sound like the book entitled, *Why Hasn't He Called?* that's because we have used it a thousand times and more. We have talked our friends heads off about why he hasn't called. It's a common question for girls).

Now, this might seems stupid to some of you because you can text your way through anything these days. I'm not trying to sound like an old fogy, but this generation texts their way through a breakup or divorce.

Rather than hearing the person on the other end of the phone and their upset voice, we text them. At this point, though, the woman wanted to make a personal contact, probably hoping that she would see him. The guy decided to call her after she made a dramatic appearance, which resulted in her putting a note on his car windshield. Well, at least she didn't egg his luxurious car.

"What are you doing putting a note on my car?" he asked her.

"I was thinking about you. I thought it was cute," she replied.

"Don't ever leave notes on my car!" he bellowed. "We're not a couple, and I don't owe you any explanation as to why I haven't called. If I decide to call you I will, but until then don't worry about it! You and I talked about this, remember?"

My guess is this guy had something to hide and she did not follow the list he gave her. He told her not to call him. "Not to call him was on his list, a list that she ignored and got her feelings hurt by dismissing it.

We want to blame the man most of the time, but we're the ones reading the wrong signal that he projects to us. His lists for her involved just having fun! "Sex". Not relationship! Not marriage!

While what's on our minds, women, is to find a potential husband. We want a relationship, baby carriage and all. This never changes, no matter how empowered we become. Then when we're hurt we will sleep with him just for the fun of it and lay our trap by getting pregnant. Well, that may not be u, okay, but there are some other man trappers out

———

there. For women, this is the most stupid way of getting what we want.

This game doesn't stop at the young women but the 30 somethings also. What was once supposed to be a pure and innocent list turns sour and bitter. The list suddenly consists of how you are going to make his life a living hell. Take note of this while you are plotting – he wants to marry the woman of his dreams and apparently it's not u.

Be careful of your planning the next time a guy asks you out. His list probably will match yours. The old saying goes why buy milk when you've got the whole cow. I say no relationship, no benefits. No ring, no benefits. That will stop all the confusion if you should keep sleeping with a guy and in return you get nothing out of it but heartache and misery. At least if you marry him, you do get all the benefits such as a home, car, bank account and you never have to worry about the kids' education and how going to make it without funds.

You are hidden for a reason and in time you will be revealed and all the explanation will be self-explanatory.

CHAPTER 6
The Confused Young Man, The Librarian and ...

One day I was at my favorite place, the library. Yes, I'm at the library a lot, shocking, I know, but it happens to be one of my favorite places to go after sitting at home pinning away on my lab top. I must admit it was my get away from all the distractions. It also gave me time to walk downtown and observe people moving in motion that reminded me of waves in the ocean.

A conversation between mother and son was taking place as they stood at the bench where I was sitting. Her son, just like any other young man who reflects today's generation through style and clothing, asked his mother about cooking dinner, but she was more concerning about him cleaning the house for a change. She lived with her son who was about thirty something and from the sound of it she had some regrets. She was divorced from her husband after 35 years and had to move in with her son until she could find a job.

"You were doing those things before I came to live with you, and now you expect me to cook and clean your house? You throw your clothes everywhere and expect me to pick up behind you. Then you say, "It's my house mom." She realizes he gets that attitude from his father. "You saw me picking up after him and now you expect the same thing. Well, I'm sorry. I'm sorry for it all. I'm sorry for giving you a poor example of a mother, or a woman. You can't expect your wife to do the same," his mother said.

"My wife. I'm not thinking about getting married," the young man said. Look what happened to you and dad. Then, he teased his mother and reminded her that he loves her. It's nothing like mom's cooking. Grandma comes over and brings me dinner!"

"That's another thing. You're taking advantage of your grandmother too."

"No, she likes doing it. She thinks that I'm not getting a proper home cooked meal," the son says sweetly. His mother looked at him in a motherly way and smiled back.

"Okay. I'll cook this time, but we will share the work from now on."

His mom explains to him she has something to do ands she'll see him later on this evening. It was as if though I could see this whole scenario playing out right before my eyes. Either that or I had a vivid imagination.

"Mom where are you going and how long you are going to be gone?"

I had a feeling she was thinking she was old enough to leave the house without him worrying about her. She felt like that child with a curfew counting down each minute she would be out. He had become overly protective of her. If I could get inside her head, I'm sure she would be saying: My son really needs to get a life, a girl, or married. Then, would begin to feel a little guilty. After all, I am the one that interrupt his life and he was just clearing the way of misplayed information that he didn't think was justifiable when he was growing up. The things I thought he wasn't paying attention to he really was and that presents a problem.

When she returns home, she can't help but noticed a pile of dishes in the sink from the night before...dishes that he left for me her wash. His clothes were thrown over the sofa and his dirty sock was on the floor next to his funky shoes and dirty underwear. She nearly blew her stack.

She mummers under her breath, "I'm not his maid and he's treating me like his father treated me.

"Mom, why didn't you answer your phone? I was worried. You were out there all alone. You don't have dad any more to protect you anymore. By the way, I made dinner. I wish you had answered, now the pizza is cold." His mother looked over and saw the pizza on the stove. Then, she looked back at him.

When he wasn't in the mood to talk, he retreated to his man-cave just like his father. *What a monster I created!* Mom thought. *What kind of husband will he make for some other woman?* She took a deep breath and smiled. He noticed that motherly look on her concerned face - That same look she give him when he was a little boy in trouble.

"Son, we need to have a serious talk."

Apparently, his mom couldn't see her own shortcomings when they all lived together as a family. This guy would turn out to be some other girl's worry in the near future if his mother couldn't help to correct the problem she had created. But, like they say, you're never too old to learn.

Finally, after observing, I walked back to the library and went to the third floor in a room called, Sights and Sounds. It has always blown me away because of the way it's designed. It had a check out desk and an information center where you could ask the nice, willing clerk to help you find everything you needed.

I was waiting for the young man who was asking the lady behind the counter questions about some videos. The handsome, but confused young man still couldn't seem to gather the information she was giving him. I wanted to interrupt them by saying to him, $1+1=2$.

Finally, he walked into the direction that she pointed out to him like a teacher pointing the direction out to her student. So, his journey begins. I snickered, and curiously walked towards the section she directed him to and saw him standing there.

Out of my peripheral vision, I saw him taking a list out of his pocket and looking at it as if he had read it a million times before. He didn't have to get familiar with the list, because it was familiar with him in a very comforting way. I could tell he was very frustrated with the list and the help he received. The lady came from the behind the counter after she saw her way clear of customers and went up to him.

I was still smiling and before she asked him about finding the movies he asked her about earlier, I got my say in. I approached him in a friendly way as the clerk handed him two of the movies he was looking for.

"You got the girlfriend's list?" I smiled,
Retuning the smile, he looked at me in a very strange way. As the short conversation continued we all laughed including the lady at the counter and a few other fence watchers.

"What's that?" he asked me.

"I'm writing a book about the very same thing you are experiencing now. Your girlfriend or fiancée has given you a list of things to do. I bet she listed every movie she wanted you to get her. She also gives you a list of things to do when you go to the grocery store.

"Yeah, she does," he said. Man, I hate the list," he said taking a deep breath. "It makes me feel like a little kid."

We both laughed while she took a quick look at the list again. He seems to be happy to accommodate his girl, but he admitted he hated the list.

How powerful is luv?
Jump in the way of it and u will c
It will knock you off your feet.
Try it
On your enemies first
If they R still standing, then it wasn't luv in the
First place.

CHAPTER 7
Get Grown Already!

Get off the bad list! If you say you're grown, then take some responsibility for yourself. Stop being so cocky with the attitude that you don't need anybody.

God even saw that Adam needed a mate. We don't live alone in this life. We are the extension of others, whether we like it or not. We are connected by association of the stems and the limbs of life that bind us.

Stop hanging around emotionally disturbed people. "The downers." Draw yourself into dealings with positive speaking, energetic people. It's hard to arrive at that level if you have been in the pits - "The piti-full way." Yes, I did separate the word and broke all the rules, because you are in a pit and full of stupid stuff.

This world is filled with subliminal messages. We're walking around like sleepy minded people. What woman doesn't want a man to take care of her? All of this, "I'm independent" nonsense has made more women lesbians. Men and women were meant

2 b life-long mates. What a pair? Not a pear something u eat and think it's good at that moment.

We can have our independence and enjoy a man 2! A man isn't something 2 b feared! He wants 2 love us like we want to luv him. He wants to take care of us, but he is afraid that your mind is too far-gone into a state of independence!

Now he has to assume the role of a little boy being raised by his mother. Who wants to argue with an independent opinionated woman? Change and Rearrange!

When a woman does complain, it's like being trap in a fiery hell! A man feels every flame of it. "Hell hath no fury like a woman scorned!" If the problem isn't resolve at that time or that evening before going to bed, she wakes up angry. It's set! The whole house on fire! When a woman is upset the whole order of the house seems to turn upside down. She draws more negative energy her way, so if I were u I would stay out of the line of fire!

The original quote for that was, "Heav'n has no rage like love to hatred turn'd nor hell a fury, like a woman scorn'd." - Act 111 of William Congreve's The Mourning Bride first produced in 1697.

One man said it feels like hell for us and that's a place I'd rather not be. Add this to your list, buddy! Opposite attracts, but why does it attract so much junk? Maybe it's the junk in us that attracts the opposite and the junk in them.

This isn't math or rocket science. We all learn it in school, but to apply it to our lives is a whole other thing. I'm sweet, but you're bitter, so put it altogether u get bitter-sweet. Good girls like bad boys! The world that our parents live in is still trying to figure this one out!

My chief concern is never learning from our mistakes, because we keep dating the guy that reminds us of the guy who reminds us of the guy, who reminds us of the guy…well,.U get the picture!

Is the lesson learned
Or should we do this dance all over again until
we get it right?
Some of us will be dancing forever if we believe in
purgatory or Ground Hogs Day (The Movie). Either way,
you're in trouble.

CHAPTER 8
Let's go to the Movies

Why are so many women going to the movies with each other or alone? This makes no sense to me. My friends asked me to go to the movies with her, and of course I said, "yes." When I got there this is what I saw, women looking more like couples. No such thing right, I know, but they did look like couples. Women in pairs! Women in groups! Women alone! Women looking lost! Women looking insecure! Where were the men? If I could answer that I wouldn't be writing this question: My reviews: Please don't make a big deal if I don't mention any of your favorite movies in my review of the movies I've seen and critiqued. I'm neither Robert Ebert and I doubt he would give a thumb's up on any of these movies I'm mentioning, nor would the new guys who are the new Robert Ebert's for that matter.

Some of my movies might be among your least favorite and that's okay. To get the list going I must talk about some of my favorite movies. They all have something to do with the list. It's either like listening to your favorite song for the first time or looking in his eyes and listening to his voice for the first time. Those things make you feel good inside and you never want that feeling go away. Even when you reach the mature age of... - Let's just say the big one. The big one means 30, 40 or 50 or when you're at that idealistic stage of your life and that giggling stage.

Movies take you into a world of make believe and the possibilities of what *if*. There are plenty of good movies out there, but keep it real. Fairytale love and fantasy are a movie delight to entertain the minds of the watchers, especially women. Fairytales aren't so far fetched. They're happening every day.

Sometimes we recognize ourselves in the movies as that person who finds real love. Most writers use real life events and experiences to write great script or to turn them into comedies. The goal is to make them less stressful than our actual current events.

I love a movie with a romantic twist to it, but it has to make sense. Well, at least the kind of sense that belongs to only me. I love romantic comedy.

Something New stars one of my favorite actors Simon Baker. The character Kenya started out in the movie by going out with her girlfriends and talking about what she wants in a man. She goes down a very precise list.

The List stars Wayne Brady, whom I've never noticed was a movie star or classified as a movie star, because I have only seen him in a few movies. I have always seen him hosting shows. By the way, he has a very good singing voice. In this movie, he was always looking for a specific woman and she had to meet all of his qualifications. He could have just as

The List stars Wayne Brady, whom I've never noticed was a movie star or classified as a movie star, because I have only seen him in a few movies. I have always seen him hosting shows. By the way, he has a very good singing voice. In this movie, he was always looking for a specific woman and she had to meet all of his qualifications. He could have just as easily solved his own problem by dating himself. I admit you must have something in common with others, but our difference is what makes us unique. That uniqueness doesn't necessarily have to make us crazy or weird.

The hero (Jamie Foxx) in the movie *Breaking All The Rules* writes a book on basic guidelines for the break up. What should and should not one do when it comes to dating? Of course the rules always
changes if a person wants to break up with you first. The movie, *Breaking All The Rules*, is about a guy who was dumped by his fiancé who realizes she just didn't want to be married and she wanted to explore her options after meeting another guy. Now, the guy she was dating was hurt. Well, yeah wouldn't you be after finding out the man you love didn't love you back? Break ups are hard to deal with. Rejection it should be called.

"You rejected me because..."

Break ups are never easy, especially when you're young and in love. It's like your whole world has ended. You can't eat or sleep. You mind gets lazy and shut down. You're angry at the world. In some cases, even the most mature men/women can't handle rejection.

Who's asking whom?

First date: If the guy is asking and taking you out it should be to his choice of movie. The both of you should watch readily unless he has asked you in the beginning what kind of movies u like. You might be surprised if you let him pick out the movie. He just might pick out a good one. Let him be in charge, so u must to learn how to follow the leader. It can only be one leader, one driver and one ship captain. This might be going against the grain, but, be like Mikey – if u "try it you might like it."

Second Date:

Which comes first, dinner or a movie…the chicken or the egghead. The rule is, it doesn't matter who does the asking. Food is a good way to start off a date anytime. Who's paying might need to be discussed before u go on the date. If he's any kind of a gentleman, he will always pick up the check. Old fashioned values go a long way. Debating interrupts the moral fiber of the dating game even on date night for adults.

KILLING THE LIST:

Can the list be killed? I don't think so. Maybe some expert opinion can tell you otherwise. Every thing starts out with the list: even yes, death. Remember we all have that pointed time. That is my opinion - that even death starts with a list.

"Who's next?" We all have asked ourselves this question, especially when people start dying in our families. Somebody is on the list before and after you. No, the list can't die, because it is as sure as death and taxes. Neither one of them will ever go away nor will one take the place of the other.

If your friend tries to kill the list, that just means he or she is trying to change something about him or herself. The list can be changed, but remember if the list changes, you change. That can be a good or bad thing, but we're hoping for good. Now that I've really got your attention, let's move on shall we?

The list will not exclude you, because u r programmed to use the list. Just don't torment the male with the list. He is also a list keeper. Although they are wired differently than the female, he's still got a list built inside of him. We just don't think about that we are living our lives this way.

Don't torment yourself everyday trying to find out what's on your list today. It is built inside of us without even thinking about it. Men are likely to be followers of the list as well as women. Men; however, see the world as it comes. Women see what's coming and expect the man 2 c it 2. Her intuition kicks in. Men will say they see it coming, but will combat the challenge through intellect.

Women get it, men don't. When men get it women don't. A woman can usually sense something is wrong, but sometimes ignores the warning.

"I like bread and butter." The man will say.

"What?" asks the woman. Don't u want some jam on that? It's better that way."

"How u going to step on my world, because I like bread and butter?"

Adaptation to each other is the key to peace and harmony. Who needs objections?

A woman's intuition is the best way of learning more about how powerful she really is and how she connects with things around her - family, friends relationships, co-workers and the whole darn planet.

CHAPTER 9
When The List Is In Love

Shakespeare wrote a cultural treasure chest and he never attended a day at a college or university. He wrote the most beautiful plays on human nature and falling or being in love. He also wrote about the dark side of man when it comes to love.

I believe the most poetic or romantic poem of all is the one that was written by William Wordsworth 1770-1850, a man who really understood sexual repression, love, heartbreak and the depression love can bring about. He understood about being young and innocent and falling in love.

"Though nothing can bring back the hour of splendour in the grass of glory in the flower,
We will grieve not rather find strength in what remains behind."

Wordsworth

Some of the greatest poems that I read in high school have faded away along with the educators who taught them. It is also the case with sonnets by other great writers such as: (Shakespeare) Hamlet's, *To Be or Not to Be*. (It might seems like it's a dooms day list for living or the dying, but the poem still spoke of love in a simple but romantic way) *Romeo and Juliet*, even *The Songs of Solomon*. The great ones!

Who taught us the true meaning of love? Whitney Houston singing about, "I will always Love U, taken from singer-songwriter Dolly Parton, 1973, Barbara Streisand's, *The Way We Were*, Maya Angelou's, *The Blacker the Berry, The Sweeter the Juice*. Who can top them on writing about love?

The book of Solomon of course! As many wives he had he would write the greatest book on love, because he loved many. In our vivid world of television and movie real love or loving someone has gotten twisted in the madness of perversion and comical imaginations. I had to go into my own memories and pull out some of the oldies but goodies. To be loved and loving someone who respects u is the greatest gift anyone can achieve and receive.

What happens when Eve encounters Adam?
Adam: strong and uncompromising
Eve: Daring and waiting for love to come

TO ADAM FROM EVE
Is it you I seek, my love, the first and the last of everything that I am and hope to be? Or is it the breath that you breathe into my soul that I need more of and no other? Or is it the image of the man who comes out of the ocean illuminating in the sun reflecting golden light of a sunset behind him with

his strong arms spreading like wings of an angel?
The water drips heavily from your body and
drenches your face like huge lumps of sweat
cascading down into a pool of unbelievable desire for
you. Maybe you are the image in my mind and
perhaps my dreams. You emerge with greatness,
taking control of my emotions completely - soft sleek,
bronze in depth, but not in fear, and darkness
without light. I remember how wonderful you were
to me, my love, my sweet.

When I felt that my feet wanted to slip from
under me as I stood on the cliff watching you walk
towards me, our eyes meet for the first time, yet I still
wanted to let go. I noticed first your swagger and
how you moved in the waves as they splashed
against the half buried rocks. Your walk was the
walk of kings and your embrace was strong and
powerful and filled me with such life, wonder, and
expectation. It was you who came to rescue me
across the ocean because my heart was troubled.

As your lips touched mine, the sweetness
intoxicated me like the grapes of your country
ripened in pureness. That new wine of wonder that
every man seeks that grows tall as trees in your
vineyard. My Adam, my love, my everything, I count
not my own selfish desire of wanting more of you. I
met such greatness when I met you. Why must I
question your gift to me? These things are much too
wonderful for me, a simple being, a woman who
longs to be loved.

What Happens When Adam encounters Eve?
Eve: Emotional runs wild

TO EVE FROM ADAM

Eve, my love, my glorious dawn, has time ceased to exist? Oh, how you showed your grace into the wings of the morning collecting all bliss and wonders. Your kisses are like expensive wine, hand picked and not touched by another. Your fragrance is intoxicating and powerful. Those who seek to love u are over come by your beauty. I am drained from the thought that no one could love me the way you do.

The dawn of you brings me joy. I feel I have failed you, and that you have never failed me, because you go into that secret place that I cannot follow. Your love reaches beyond the sky in the great beyond that my mind cannot comprehend. Neither can my eyes behold such beauty. My ears have not heard such lovely words that have entered my heart.

Your heavenly body is surrounded by good things and cultivated into perfection, the kind that is precious and that my heart desires. Upon your head is a crown of love, priceless of all jewels that are upon the earth. Brand me with your fingertips upon my heart, so I may not consider another. I will remember how kind you were to me in my times of trouble. You left an imprint upon the depths of my soul.

Your smile was like the sunshine upon my face, bathing me into happiness. What I say to other without risking ruins. If I tell the truth, the whole world will split open. U r my first and last, whom I shall want 4 ever. You are about as close to Heaven as I can get without my mind going completely insane. Your greatness is 2 wonderful for me, a simple being...a man who longs to be loved by you.

With this, will Adam feel the same way about Eve when their love seems so final in terms of eternity? Will they both write each other sonnets and
sing songs of love? Will they grow apart as "memories light the corners of their minds?"

Final Goodbyes
Write me something soft that will remind me of your virtue
Something that will capture innocent moments I spent with u.
Something as gentle as spring and full of excitement that will never go away
Write me something warm that will snug me on a winter's day.
Write me something secretive as a whisper in one's ear
Ringing out the sound of sweet nothing I can cherish in a new year.
Something as precious as life itself in a golden setting of the sun
As tears lie wet on luscious grass at the break of dawn.
A flower of remembrance, oh how I kept
In my heart endless times of moments of emotions swept.
Sun-filled days overflowing with wishes
Kissing the blue skies with kisses.
I don't want to lose those precious moments, you see,
So please, my love,
Write to me.

*If the songs won't get u the music will!

CHAPTER 10
The Teen Thing

The forgotten list

If only I could feel this way again. Parent's really are funny when it comes to teen love as if they were never teens before or they just don't want to face the fact that Romeo (their son) and Juliet (somebody else's daughter) will one day feel the passion and the fiery darks of cupids arrow, which causes falling in love.

It is flamed by hot blood that pumps through our veins and pulsation into a burning sensation of passion! It is by far the most important feeling that humans will ever feel for each other.

R u a teenager? Well if u are not you probably wish u were. You might say, "I'm glad those days r long gone!" You don't want to feel the excitement because time had a calling card on your youthful life. That was fun and crazy time for some and for others, a time of embarrassing moments and horrible experiences. It was the time of virtue, a time of innocence, a time of giggles when a cute boy or girl walked by, a time of confusion about our bodies, a time of growing pains, a time when mom was mom, and dad was dad and u could tell the difference, a time of caring hands.

What I loved about being a teenager for the most part was being free without worries. You didn't have to worry about grown up things, but now kids do. It was a time when the media exposed, "the single mom." It was also a time when thousands of single dads raised their children as well as moms. If you look at some of the old television shows you would hear on *My Three Sons*, starring Andy Griffith, the song that had Americans singing along. *People Let me Tell U About My Best Friend*, Eddie Courtship, and *Different Strokes*: If neither mom nor dad were there, everyone else pitched in to help. If mom was the one that ran away, we pitched in and helped dad without complaining, because it was the way things were.

If mom had to work two jobs, the big kids took care of the little kids and no one called CPS.
When we were in high school, socialization was a big part of our lives and it was important to be on that list even if it meant going against your better judgment or being dumped on by others who were also trying to become apart of the list.

Being a teen caused us to get into some uncomfortable situations. For the most part, though, they were fun-filled days! What the older generation called "the good ol' days".

Today, either you remember or don't want to remember the romance - how his voice sounded so sweet like he was reciting poetry in your ear. How you stayed up all night talking on the phone and didn't want to say goodbye and days when moms or dads stayed up worrying when you were on your first date.

Remember that first glance at a boy? Or maybe that first glance at a girl? Butterflies fluttered in your stomach when he/she came near you. Or how about the boy you liked really liked someone else, and you were angry with the girl instead of him? Now, it all seems so silly. He wasn't really worth fighting over. You're glad you weren't the girl that chased after him, because she's unhappy and filled with tears.

Nothing has really changed when it comes to teenage love. It's like coming home for Christmas. That "Christmassy" smell that enters your sensors when you first walk into the house and the feel of warmth all around you helps you to imagine that the fireplace is lit when you know you don't have one. You might remember the smell of baked pies filled the air, and presents under the oversized tree that dad picked out. Well, maybe you had a simple Christmas without the entire trimming, still the feeling was there. That year u remembered that you didn't get the toys you wanted or no toys at all, but mom was mom and comforted u with love and hugs.

They giggle! They smile! Sky Rocket in Flight! It was like fire works over and over again off in your head. That excitement! That zeal for love - that wonderful feeling of being in love. You can't breath; because he/she takes ur breathe away! You're deliriously in love. All you do is think about each other, and write his/her name a million times. Your knees are weak! Palms are sweating! You can't wait to see each other when it was only hours ago that you saw each other.

For guys the thrill of the chase and for girls getting caught. Holding hands! Everything you did had a meaning. This was a time when a fight was a fight between cats and dogs or just cats, no guns, no putting your car on flats or breaking windshields and killing your whole family. A flirt was a flirt!

Songwriters have written songs about it, and greatest poets can't count the ways. King Solomon was a fool over it. The greatest king of pop even wrote about it. Shakespeare crowns it with his greatest piece, *Romeo and Juliet*. The man above shows His greatness through it. In Italy, guys could still get away with pinching a woman's behind and not being offensive.

Love is like a flower in the spring we are just happy that we got a chance to experience it.
Love is pure and it's never fails and it can be tainted by humans point a views.
We sing in our hearts
We cry a river of tears
We recite poetry 2 sooth or hearts
We read sonnets and remember old
Songs that reminds us of how it use to be.
We don't want to forget
We scream so we can't go insane
We still crave
Nvrmnd the Leftovers
Late-Life Love
Leftovers syndrome

If you think you're too old, well think again. An author by the name of Connie Goldman wrote these words in her book *Late-Life-Love*.

"Late-life come with leftovers adult children, grandchildren, health concerns previous living situations, sexual expectations, financial discrepancies, divorce, care giving, experiences, grief and loss."

These are some of the things u can expect, but when ur twenty something or thirty something we don't think about any of this. Connie Goldman has a way of preparing you for love, because it's not over until "the fat lady sings!" And she might just keep singing until she's 90 years old according to Dr. Ruth.

When u think about it, 30 is going down hill. Turning 30! At thirty u feel young, but you know you're not getting any younger and the younger they are, the better they guys like them. You don't have that snap back body anymore. You have to work it to keep it.

You can talk to someone older who knows about reinventing yourself and relationships. You can't be the same person at the age thirty that you r in your twenties. You can't be the same person when you r forty something that you were when u were in your thirties. Not even when it comes to having good sex. Sometimes women have to guide a man through what they want in order to feel simulated again. You r no longer that energetic person u use to be. Now is the time for trying sometime new. When ur young, you go through the motion of having sex and with it comes these good and exciting feelings. Now, you just want someone to hold u and tell u that they care, so sex is still important but stimulation of again. You r no longer that energetic person u use to be. Now is the time for trying sometime new. When ur young, you go through the motion of having sex and with it comes these good and exciting feelings. Now, you just want someone to hold u and tell u that they care, so sex is still important but stimulation of the mind becomes more in a securing way. The teen feeling doesn't have to end, but it must mature. Looking back is okay, so u can relax and mature with grace.

The Woman's list:

Y were females born with the list? I don't have the answer to that question. The great Oz has it, so don't go looking over the rainbow. I do know that we have a list for everything. The man has one 2. It's just hard to get him to admit that there is a list. The *so-called* list is like the world's greatest kept secret to them. Unlike women, they share it with their male counterparts.

Getting married and having children are the very first things on a woman's list. We play these games when we're little girls. The guy doesn't know it. I mean, he doesn't really know what the game is all about. We use them in the game by playing husband and wife and grooming them for what's to come in the future. They (our mothers,) groom us for. They tell us the fairytale of life, even though it might seem backward. Why can't they just say that one day a guy will be looking for a wife and it might just be you?

"One day you'll grow up and find a man just like your father...One day you'll grow up and find the man of your dreams...One day you'll grow up and get married to a wonderful man."

They never tell us that one-day we'll get married and of how we should face tough discussions that will go against everything that we were taught.

The House list:
There is always a house list and it can go on forever! But, don't expect a man to like your flowery castle as much as you don't like his wooden den.
Bring something to the table that you both can enjoy - even in the bedroom.

The wedding list:
U c, we start the wedding list before we get engaged or make out invitations. We don't even invite the guy into this dream world of ours. We dream him up and make out a tangible list of his qualities. Sometimes, we just write down what we want leading up to the big day. Men don't do this and I doubt they even think about it. They don't sit around the house thinking of a to-do list and dreaming about getting married. They don't worry about the kind of tux they will be wearing or that kind of stuff. When it comes closer to time, then they decide.

Sometimes, we can be pretty biased and ridiculous about the list. We want a tall, dark, and handsome guy with money and a nice, expensive car. We want to marry a millionaire. (C body odor) This is like brushing your teeth without any kind of toothpaste or back up plan on how you're going to keep your breath fresh. We don't consider the gems or food in between our teeth. We don't even take notice of the fact that we don't have healthy gums.

We don't apply mouthwash or floss. You say to yourself, "I just want to marry a millionaire and a cute looking guy so I can have cute kids." Be careful what u wish for. You just might get it and it will come in a pretty packaged box with a surprise in it.

Bridesmaids list:
- To-do-list
- Engagement list
- Invitation list
- Party list
- Vacation list
- Clothing list
- Grocery list
- Laundry list
- Appointment list
- PMS
- Cramps back abdominal fatigue
- Dating list (The dating list is a whole different ball game when it comes to young love.
- (Recap The teen thing) Then u have this kind of list:
  a. "I hate u list"
  b. "Ur not coming to my party list"
  c. "She's not invited"
  d. "I don't like u exclusive list"
  e. "The girls I don't like list""
  f. "The girls I won't find dead with list"
  g. "The boys I won't find dead with list"
  h. "I don't hang out with girls who's prettier than I am list
  I. "I'll never fix in or be good enough
  J. "I love u...you love me not

No geeks/nerds allow (Oh, you got to love this one, because might as well get used to calling them tomorrow rulers. They are the smartest and will someday be the Presidents, great scientists, astronauts, work in intelligence, doctors, lawyers, make great discoveries, and a whole lot of other things I can't name. They will have the highest paying jobs on the planet. Let's not forget the creative nerd with special effects, genius of things my tiny little mind – things it can't comprehend or think about or pronounce. Yeah, they are the geniuses "brainiacs!"

- "The ugly list"
- "I don't ever want to c u again list.
- "U makes me sick list"
- "Avoiding list (I will avoid u at any cost)
- "I want ur man and I will get him list"
- "The cheaters list." (Who I'm cheating on and Y)

A man said to me, "The woman want smooth relationship they will follow along with the list, especially the honey-do list. Women better learn that a man is not guided by his feelings. They need a tangible thing to guide them along the way." The right kind of woman:

"I'll love a woman who sleeps around, but I don't ever want her for my wife."

Pretty girl list:

Don't ever get on the pretty girl list. You'll will be hated and envied even when you are getting older. The un-pretty is always fearful that she will never be as pretty as the pretty girl. She is right. Things come much easier for pretty girls and harder for those that don't have the killer body and pretty face. I don't know if this pertains to a job situation, because women want to strike them down like lighting. Society has proven this time and time again, and tries to make up for it by having an overweight girl with simple looks on a movie or TV show.

Pretty is as pretty does. A pretty girl does get more attention. We love looking at their pretty faces. Women seem to comment more than men.

The Good list and bad list:

A good list should consist of two things: You and I, and not a baby makes three by using trickery. If ur mommy never told u, I'm telling u it never works. That's why they made condoms for males and all kinds of birth control for females.

"The condoms break," someone said to me.
This I do know, but without me sounding like ur mom, u should be on some kind of protection plan, and then u won't have to worry about breakage or leakage, now would u?

The good list comes with love, respect, guidance, instruction, direction, good attitude and most of all patients. You won't scare the guy and maybe he'll call back the next time around.

The list is not meant to control, and everything around u. Do you always have to have the last word? If you do, something is wrong with u! If u meet a controlling person, run! They will control the relationship and u. They are controlling and unbearable, and yes although we love them we want out! It's good to have a little control, but we often abuse the power. That's how we come up with words like "control freak!"

You are on the list of many others without even realizing it. Yeah, it's that funny. We may not even think about it, but we are on somebody's list. The Entertainment magazine calls it a hit list. The guy who talks about everybody's clothing has his own list. *ET* (*Entertainment Tonight*) calls it the worst dressed list, and in our own community wherever it is, we call it the gossip list.

Somebody somewhere is talking about people they don't even know or aren't hardly acquaint with and don't even give them the time of day. We're on the social list. We're not invited because we haven't proven ourselves worthy of the company of others who own the list.

We invite people over to a gathering or social setting because we want to be the talk of the town. If you're wondering why you're the one who's never invited, it's because ur not on the list. Who wants to be on the list? Well, all of those who r not popular or worthy to be in the company of others who think they are more than u. Maybe you don't seem to be the social butterfly that everybody is talking about and wants to be in your circle. They want you to volunteer or to be there, but not really a part of them.

The Unrealistic List:
Chances are it will never happen, but if u wish upon a star who knows it just might fall. I call this the *rescue me list.*

We dream of men who are movie stars and other heart throbs like them. We may not ever meet these guys: Realistically, they are already taken by other beautiful movie stars with status that we may not ever achieve, but then we just might be in the right place at the right time.

Having a movie star romance?

We dream of the romances like u see in the movie, where the hero rescues the damsel in distress, even though we know wishing upon a star is for little girls in pink little dresses. The Prince rides on the white horse and a prince eventually meets his princess. The Royals of England we praise in far away place where true love and fairytales do come true. Little girls are encouraged to dreams dream of hopes of one day they, too, will be rescued.

Wishing upon a star doesn't seem so far fetched after all. The irony is they were true stories, but made into fairytales for us dream to keep dreaming about until our day arrives or doesn't arrive. We all r dreaming the dream and never stepping out on faith and dreaming seems more practical: Your prince will come, because it can happen.

The irony is the boy wants to be the prince. He wants to be seen as the hero's that wins the girl's heart or who rescues her. We need a hero, but when he comes, he often finds barriers like ATTITUDES. (See the chapter Dance with Me)

Just the other day, I was talking to a couple of 20-year-old girls who were roommates.

"What r u looking for in a guy?" I asked them.

They looked at each other and laughed, of course. I thought to myself they are so young and probably don't know what they want right now. Our ideas about guys get better with time. You will know when you have learned that hard lesson on love and who to love.

"Sometimes, he fights his case. He will tell me he knows the better route than I do. He will stick to it. He won't move. I'm saying, I get off at 6:45 and to pick me up. He'll be there at 7:00 o'clock. Let it be on the other foot," one girl said to me.

The girl's friend said to me with a hint of seriousness to her voice. She had been waiting for her fiancée' to pick her up from work.

"Why are you late? " I asked him.

"It's only 7:00 o'clock," he answers me smiling.

"I had better not show up late or we will be fighting about it

all night long. I learn not to argue with him."

The first young woman's mouth was wide open as she begins with a long one word, "I."

"I don't know any other way to handle my boyfriend. That's one thing I can't stand is fighting with someone who doesn't respect my point of view. It takes him three days to do what I want him to do. I have to constantly remind him. It's really irritating and annoying at times. I just leave him to the dogs!"

I didn't even ask her about what leaving him to the dogs meant. It was far over my head. Once they started talking, I can tell they had some difficulties, but in time can be easily resolved. I just wanted to laugh and say wait until they grow up which seems still impossible for men to do.

"I don't want him to take all day to pick up his stupid, smelly shoes off the floor." Stop putting your stupid, stinky, shirt on the sofa when you come into the house. I just leave them there and eventually he does pick them, because the smell alone will become unbearable! I have to remind him that I'm not his mother."

Some Truths:

Truth be told, a woman really doesn't want a male perspective. Sure, we say we do, but it terrifies us 2 know what they r really thinking. When he offers his opinion we want to rip his head off. We r afraid of the obvious, "he really thinks and feel this way." The scariest thing is trying to figure him out, just like us just when u think you know them. You get the picture. We really don't want a male perspective about a relationship, because we think we already know what he should be thinking and feeling. Most of the time it's our way or the highway! If he crosses that line on the list he's in big trouble. Yet, we are the ones who pushes for answers and so eagerly to know how he really feels. Once we hear the answer we get upset. Is that fair?

Clarification of Dogs and Pigs and other known animals

Usually, if it eats and acts like a pig, smell like a pig, it's usually a pig. Sometimes it's our own blindness that keeps us from seeing that yeah, he's a pig. If he chases like a dog, barks like a dog, and acts like a dog, he's a dog! Yeah, he's a dog! It's seems that some men are better off being dogs.

"If he's a dog he's a dog, and I don't care if it's my brother he's a dog too. I don't care if he's my father, he's a dog too!" a girl said to me. Clearly she has some anger issues going on there. (See the section on Pitch Out)

Yeah, he acts like the teenager that u met a long time ago, He won't change! He might just like who he is right now. It's up to u to get ready for the long haul. Can u live with it or not? We get frustrated! We get furious! We break it off! Or we end up marrying the pig with the dog attributes and the immature behavior that we fell in love with. If u tolerate the craziness now, you'll tolerate it later.

Why r we keeping people on our list of like u r not? Get a life and most definitely get a back-up plan.

CHAPTER 11
What are boys made of?

Your mom probably has repeated the nursery rhyme to u like her mother repeated to her. (This poem appeared in a manuscript of English Poet Robert Southey 1774-1843 Wikipedia)

What are boys made of?
Frogs and snails and puppy-dogs' tales
That's what little boys are made of.

Then your grandmother or great grandmothers probably used "Snips and snail's and puppy dogs' tails." What ever the case may be, the poem is for any generation during that time.

What are little girls made of?
Sugar and spice and everything nice.

Today's girls would probably disagree with this cute little poem. They would probably say that boys are made of all sort of crazy things and girls aren't as nice as they use to be.

——

Georgie Porgie Pudding and pie kiss the girls and made them cry...well, Y? is it because he stole a kiss or that he made them feel so good they had to cry.

Some women have such low opinions about men. The things we hear on talk shows and radio shows is unbelievable! Men aren't all that bad. If they r why do we want them? The world wouldn't b the same without a strong man at our sides and it wouldn't be the same without a strong woman at his side. Our conversations surely wouldn't b as delightfully colorful. What on earth would we talk about? We couldn't talk about how badly we r being treated. We love to talk about them and they are the subjects of most of our conversations.

You know, I think we truly love them. If u have one u had better get used to him, because one day you might just be a mother to these so called women chasers, no good for nothing, lazy, no child support paying men. They are the objects of our affection! And without them there would be nothing else for us to talk about. Well, nothing quite as interesting.

There are some good possibilities out there. When we keep thinking negative we bring more negative things to us such as no good guys in our lives. If we keep thinking that men are all are no good, Mr. Right will be seen as Mr. Wrong.

We need men to keep society going. I don't think I want to live in a world where there are no men. Without a man, we can't reproduce...This is not just a sad thing and a bad thing, it is the true. People who prefer the opposite sex find themselves lacking something, the joy of motherhood or fatherhood, and that's why they are always trying to adopt and screaming to society that they can be good parents. I have no doubt that two caring people, even if they are wrapped up in the wrong packing, can make good parents.

We need both males and females to make reproduction happen. This is the truth, like it or not! It takes two to make a baby. They don't come from a funny farm! This is why sex is so private and should be explicated like everything else in life especially to young adults. No one wants to know that mom and dad once had sex and you find it totally disgusting.

"I love men all kinds of men," one woman stated. If they are handsome then I give them their props. If they are good citizens I give them their props. If they are regular Joes I give them their props. Even the drunk on the street.... he wasn't born a drunk. He was somebody's child just like I am. He had to be born of a man and woman. Unless you believe in some other life form that formed them out of sea and he grew legs one day and walked upon the earth."

Pitch out:

Pitch out the bad relations and experiences we had when we first fell in love. Pitch out everything you have ever hear about men. Pitch out "they all are dogs?" And they don't do tricks on ur comman. But on the other hand, if u give him a bone he just might. LOL.

If they all are dogs why are we the ones that's chasing them down! Don't be in the chaos! Believe in a man's abilities again. Pitch out the idea that u hate men and encourage them so that the can be better leaders, and to be better fathers. Pitch out the idea that "they all are power hungry freaks!" Pitch out the idea that "they all are creepy, who creeps, and weirdoes to be watched."

Pitch out the idea "I can do it all my self." You will just work that much harder. If we can do it all by ourselves we won't need, child-support, food stamps, the soup line, homeless shelters, extract money from mom, dad and grandma.

This is a bunch of stereotypical social nonsense. I've said this before with subliminal messages. Do like Olivia Newton John in Grease, tell them they *"better wake up because u need a good man."*

Pitch out the idea that you're a queen and you need no king. Stop putting men in a box and grouping them with the guy who has hurt u. We c that same guy over and over again in each date and relationship we get into. Is it because we keep dating the same guys that remind of some good quality that he had? Then, when we get disappointed, we want to blame the guy instead of blaming ourselves.

Would you call yourself stupid? Yes or no? Would you call yourself desperate? Yes or no? An honest person will admit when he or she is wrong. Now the question is, how honest are you?

Man's blue print - A recognizable force of leadership

Men, complexity is less than a woman, but equally matched when it comes to getting the job done. He goes through self-examination daily, something that a woman could never understand. He resents the fact that women want a duplication of themselves in him.

The common theory
We r driving each other to make decisions that are not good for either of us, the male and the female. This makes me think that this is why men are turning themselves into women. The pressure alone drives men up the wall. Waiting makes them more sensitive. It enters their psyche that they should act more like a woman and think more like a woman. Even Steve Harvey entitled his book *Act like a Lady Think Like a Man*. Sometimes, the thinking gets misconstrued and this is why we have this ball of confusion. We do too much because we are wired wrong. Yet, his book is a good tool for women to understand a man.

The most perfect person…well, we'll soon found out
We weren't perfect at all.
Yeah, I mean, we who always think we r the perfect ones
and that everyone else was born with a defect.

CHAPTER 12
To Boldly Go Where No Man Has Gone Before

I heard someone say, "Warn your mom not to read it." Don't u know that ur mother was born before u and has already read everything and seen every thing that u r now experiencing. Nothing will come as a shock to her, but it's good to pretend that you've never seen it or heard it and that's the game they will still play privately with their grown children.

Masturbation is it a no or go?
A boy has wet dreams
A girl masturbates
No matter how harsh it seems
A girl participates
A boy ejaculates and ejaculates

No one wants to put this on the list, but girls are now talking about it and are not shy about using the big Masturbation. This word and doing the act has the clearance of all the medical world and talk shows. We used to whisper the word sex or when a girl gets her period for the first time. Where has the modesty gone? Not anymore! Anything goes with this generation who seems to have no respect for each other.

If a child/teen were caught masturbating they were consider evil. They became tormented souls and the evilness of it needed to be cast out of them. The children were once thought up as filled with all kind of lustful spirits.

Some might say the children would wind up getting warts on their hands and bad acne. It was just plain nasty! If you mess with something too long something is bound to not work right in that department. The feel and the affect of another human touch may not excite you, because you are experiencing something that's unnatural to the human body - another human touch.

Sleepovers with young people usually results in their talking about masturbating - even among college students. Some people aren't even aware that they are doing it until one night they wake up touching themselves in the heat of the moment.

Some say our self-conscious has slipped into our dreams. Most parents don't want to talk about it because then they would have to take a look at themselves during those embarrassing moments. They have become the adults and adults just don't wake up in a cold sweat with the hands in an intimate position on their private parts. Get over yourself! It happens to the best of us – even those who consider themselves perfect little angels.

When they are not having sex they are having, wet dreams and masturbating becomes a parent's nightmare.

Jack and Jill:

It's no secret when a girl and a guy are going out on a date. Or the cool words, "Date Night," 4 adults. We have some idea of what's going on with our bodies and why it is reacting like an eruptive volcano in the middle of the night.

We don't ever like to think of it this way, but a young man probably never will tell u what happens to him as a young man. He will share it with another young man.

This was such a private conversation even I didn't want to talk about it. A young man with Tahitian skin, warm stares, and one raised eye-brow approached me about a horrible experience when he was 16 years old. I didn't think there was anything horrible about it after all it was an act of nature. I will call these this encounters of Jack and Jill.

"I was about fifteen when it happened to me." I woke up with sticky stuff all over me. I yelled out to my mom and I told her something was happening to me. My father was never home, so the answers came from my mom. I wasn't embarrassed; I was just hoping I wasn't turning into some kind of alien or something. My mother smiles in a motherly manner as she usually does and told me about what was happening to my body. This isn't something that she prepared me for. She told me about using condom if the time comes when I wanted to have sex. That's all! She preached about protection, and respecting a girl's body. She never talked about me being me covered with something that came from out of my own body. It freaked me out!"

Then after she gently explained to me that I had had a wet dream, she talked to my older brother who took me aside and gave me a heart-to-heart and man-to-man talk. I was surprised that it happened to him and that it happened to all young men some even younger than I was.

I am grateful so now when I do marry and have children of my own children, I'll know what to tell them! Thanks mom! I was just grateful that it wasn't something I was doing to make this happen to my body. I am also grateful that I had an understanding mother who didn't laugh at me. I never talked to my girl about it, I'm still too embarrassed. It's something that I would share with a friend, because guys definitely joke about it, and the girl won't understand. If I get teased, at least I'll be with the guys."

Next, I will call this girl Jill. One day Jill said to me, "I'm a church girl. I wouldn't dare tell my mom that I had been masturbating. No way! Could you imagine the look on her face? I would be like the segment in your book what we talked about when u first did this interview. She would be trying to cast a lust demon out of me. My mother thinks I'm perfect and I let her think it. I did stay a virgin all through high school, but when I went to college I met a guy that I really liked and one night it just happened. I wasn't a virgin any more until this day. I never told my mother. Some of my friends have confessed to me that they have masturbated. We don't know why our bodies want sex, but it does and it seems to me that it is natural."

I will call this the second girl Mara. "Mastur-bation is better than a heart break," one of my friends said to me. At least you don't have to worry about someone calling you names at school or at the wall where we hang out. I heard grow folk call each other sluts. She was a slut in high school she gave it up to everybody." That stuck on my mind. You won't get teased, because it happens in your own private world and you don't have to share it with anybody."

Is masturbating a sin or a kin?

I think - and this is just my opinion, if a person thinks that he can use masturbation like a drug addict to his addiction then it's wrong to do. If you feel that you don't need a man to please u and that u can please yourself through getting off like some pervert who looks through windows to satisfy his needs, then you are wrong. If you use masturbation in a perverted way, you are wrong and can easily be mistaken as a pervert who is only mastering your world in an unrealistic way.

One thing about masturbating is that you'll never get pregnant from it and it will give u a false sense of stimulation. Your body might only respond to masturbating. When u do finally find a good mate, you may never really enjoy the beauty of lovemaking again. Surveys say that virgins, whether young or old have ejaculated or masturbated once in their lifetime. Even if u abstain from sex for a long period of time, whether it is voluntarily or involuntarily, you can be triggered by a sex dream. If you are pleasing yourself too much, you will be hard to please in bed.

When u c the glass is half empty, it could really be that we c what we want to see and we think what we want to think. Try to see the glass as half full.

Married couples masturbating and ejaculating
Perversion or Conversions?
Or just plain someone has to take care of ur needs!
The real Grown Up question
Some gross situations
You may want to skip this part
You may not want to read this part
You may want to ask your spouse/friend this question: Are you masturbating?

Should married couples be doing it? Not with each other, but off by themselves. All I have to say is this: When u get sexual pleasure elsewhere, it is a matter of someone not doing his or her job at home. This means if u r using your own sexual devices or your hand in the middle of the night. I have read books on married people who would rather ejaculate or masturbate than to cheat on their spouse. Isn't this a form of cheating? "It's a pretty sticky situation," like the young man said. No pun intended. Really, what's happening to married people who are finding themselves masturbating rather than having regular sex with their spouses? Isn't this the craziest thing u ever heard?

One woman told me something and I was too afraid to return any comment. I felt really embarrassed when she said it. She talked as if the conversation was just as natural as the sun rising each morning. I just don't know how some people let words just flow out of their mouths without batting an eyelid. Wow! What a colorful statement that I will never forget? When u think nothing can shock u it can.

"If he's not taking care of me, I'll take care of

myself," she said laughing. "I've got vibrators and oil. I take care of myself," she said continuing to laugh. "It happens to the best of us...masturbating, because our bodies crave sex once we had it. The desires burns in us so we want sexual satisfaction. If I have to satisfy myself, I will. Sometimes I do wake up and not knowing I'm doing it."

Just be careful how u treat u body - even it has limits. The way the media and talk shows have distorted the truth with their subliminal messages, we hardly know what the truth is. It's no longer what your parent's want for you, but what they say is happening and what u should be aware of and doing.

I think anything can harm you body if it's not presented in the right fashion or form, and if it's not taught right. You can abuse your own body as well as poison somebody else's mind. You decide. What is acceptable and what's not acceptable? In this case why would u want 2 tell anybody what u do, because once they have the information you can be the target of name calling or the subject on the internet. If you are doing it, keep it to yourself. What don't people understand about invasion of privacy?

People have some nasty labels out there. They'll either call you a sick-o, or pervert or just wait to stick it to u. They will think something is wrong with you and that your mind is very sick. If you are doing it and doing it too much, keep it to yourselves. Think of it this way. Girls share a lot especially when they are involved in book clubs, slumber parties, and the girls nights out. They talk about things just like boys. Sometimes they share about what they did to their significant others and sometimes it's just between girls.

The Code of Honor:
The line is drawn between men and women. Women want men to share what they do when they go out with the boys, and they don't want to share, because of feeling judged by the female. This is an invasion of the man code. A young man doesn't want to tell his fiancée what he had on the last day of being a single man. No matter how much the girl wants to know. Why should he? Why does the girl keep insisting he tells her like in the movies? It's the "don't ask, don't tell" policy with men. He does leave things out. It's in the male code - "The dude" code. The bachelor party reveals the man code. Men would rather make up stuff than let us into their world.

"What happens in Vegas stays in Vegas." The movies *Hanger* and *Best Man*. Why do the women torment themselves into panic mode? We all need to look back on life and laugh about something we have done that was weird or stupid without feeling depressed about it.

My Xes.
Sometimes Sex can turn into xes (spelled backwards for punning purposes)
Loose as a goose and can't be tied down. One thing about sex, when ur young it can be heartbreaking, so if ur parents don't want u to have it, it's because they are trying to keep u from a lot of heartbreaks and leaving behind a trails of exes.

Most males don't want a girl that has been around the corner more than two times. Men don't like to date women who have dated more than they have. They are considered on the fast track and will sleep with anyone. They are not trustworthy because they see dating as having sex with everybody who takes them to a dinner and a movie.

Having too many exes means he won't be able to hold ur attention. He can't ever measure up. Many times when we do have many exes, we tend to throw it in our partner's face and compare him/her with the exes. Is that fair? No, but we do it all the time.

If you wish someone was more like your ex you shouldn't be with that person. Apparently ur ex doesn't want to be bothered with you and that's why you are on the ex's list.

Real love became tainted or better yet an emotional wreck for u, and you are experiencing what I call "old women's syndrome". You might experience the good with the bad of maturing into a real adult, or you could experience loneliness, anxieties, fear, bitterness despair and insecurity.

Look in the mirror, because you might be coming down with the case of the old woman syndrome. It's apart of growing whether you are a male or female. This is the thing about love or falling in love.

- Choleric Bossy/the leader type
- Melancholy, creative, realistic
- Sanguine - don't like to keep schedules, free-spirited
- Phlegmatic - laid back family oriented

DON'T MESS WITH MOM!

"I couldn't dare tell my mom about sex. She would throw the Bible at me and then tell me a horror story about burning in hell for on night of pleasure. Remember the movie Carrie? Well, that's my mom. Seriously! She will scream out, "You're in sin! You're going to hell! You're body isn't made for fornication! You're bought with a price!" She will go on and on! I never told my mother when I first had sex! She scares me!" the girl said.

Sweet Nothings

Feeling good comes with a price. When it feels too good to be true it probably is! It's a heart throbbing thing that beats with every hand holding walk. The rhyme of the sound of music in your inner ear become like a poetic, pulsating piece from your heart to ur head.

You don't need a picture to capture precious moments, because pretty soon you'll be deleting them or ripping them throwing them in the trash! They will be also put in boxes or albums, untouched, or tucked away with every other forgotten thing.

Delusion or Conclusion:

Those moments are like one of our favorite romantic movies that some how we think defies how our feelings. At least wishing that was us, especially during those girly, breakup, dramatic, lonely days. (Refer back to the chapter The Women Thing - We Will Never Conquer)

You know, when we feel like eating a whole box of chocolates or ice and bon, bons, not thinking about the calories, cholesterol, heart choking, pound adding to our hips food. We don't want to remember who's sweeping who off their feet. All we do is think about that broom we bought for him, and that you should have kept it to clean your own house. For good reason of course, because we will be doing most of the sweeping after we have been swept off our feet by love. We just can't get right thinking we're a part of something bigger than ourselves. We should listen to the warning signs: This person is not the one. We r wrapped up, and caught up - caught up in a delusion that we are indeed living in a fantasy. If u want to get caught up in the rapture, look for real love. The total essence in all of this is the deepest combination that we will ever feel - love.

Exercising the Whole U

I get tired of hearing that a little exercise won't kill you. Can't they say something else? This will make you want to erase the word exercise out of the dictionary, but some genius though it would be good for all of us to know. Diets don't fail people, people fail diets! It takes will power! It takes hard work! A lot of people fail to go through with diets!

My great brilliant suggestion is this: See a doctor first before you get into some extreme exercising. Make it fun! Walk it off! Walk for your health! Get a friend involved so you won't have to do it alone. If u have kids, get them involved in walking with u! Get ur neighbor involved! Just do it and don't count it as a chore or something you just have to do. That's no fun!

You have to create an atmosphere of fun, because exercising is intimidating enough. You don't want to make yourself have to do it. Now, if you can't walk far don't beat yourself up about it! Do some strolling along the way and hum a tune. Drink plenty of water. Throw the soda out and starve your craving. Slowly wean yourself off of eating too many sweets. Just don't quit cold turkey because you might not have the will power to stop eating sweets. Then, when you feel that you have let yourself down, you go back eating more and more! Now you're depressed about ever starting the diet in the first place. When they say mind over matter, it's true.

You mind isn't this big giant control center that wants you 2 b like a robot. You are in control. Your body shouldn't tell u what 2 do. U should tell your body what to do. Do as I command u.

Rather than thinking of it this way, change your way of thinking and then you'll hear it say something different.

"I am here to serve you. I will follow your directions." What do you want to do today?"
We love to eat meat! We love to eat junk! We love to eat sweet!

If we learn to control our eating habits and the way we eat our bodies will act younger and feel so good with all the endorphins that sets our mind and body on a natural high! Walking more! More life! More energy! More great sex! Yeah, we all like that one. Sometimes, the things we eat can make us feel sluggish. Our brain lacks oxygen and we have to ask ourselves what r we doing wrong? Every time we go get groceries you might see a sign that says, "Eat me!" All the wrong foods are calling out to you. U see foods that are healthy for you saying the same thing, but in a different way, "Hey, come over here, I'm a delicious piece of fruit. I'm green, I'm a vegetable. Please buy more of me."

I'm not telling you to go vegan, or become a vegetarian. It' was mama who said, "Eat your vegetables", and boy, was she right.

If you try to eat more vegetables and fresh fruits and eat fewer sweets, your body will feel super great! Yeah, and you will lose some of that weight that you have been screaming about! Yeah, screaming! You're screaming at people, because you're on some kind of crazy diet that's got you running around about in the house acting crazy.

At home and at work, you're just biting people's heads off for no apparent reason, and if you do have what you consider a good one you don't want to bit their heads off because it may not make tasty meal afterwards. When you practice eating healthier, you will reap the benefits of a healthier life.

Don't fry! Bake! Try Boil! Try grilled! Remember, your mom was right about eating your vegetables. Getting proper rest is sometimes hard to do.

If you walk before going to bed, you'll have a restful night. The same with exercising before you go to bed. Don't even think about letting the TV put you to sleep. That is not a good sleep aid. Your dreams are interrupted, so turn it off! There is a time 4 every thing and your time is to feel better about living and making your body feel good with you!

Exercise your mind to thinking good thoughts! Keep your mind clean always from toxic thoughts!

I just heard the craziest thing. A woman had gained so much weigh she tilted the scale and she blames it on her husband having an affair. Man! What low self-esteems and then to blame it on her husband and to have her husband thinking she weighs a ton because of me. How sad! There are a lot of things I could say about this situation, but I won't dare. I don't want a lot of overweigh people writing and telling me about why I said what I said.

From my own experience my husband had an affair and I found out there are a lot of other ways to vent and eating myself into an early grave wasn't one of them. That goes for guys 2! Who will love u better than ur self? Not mom, dad, brother or sister, loving u is the key of getting over any situation and finding something bigger than u. Do u really think the next guy wants this big of a challenge of nursing you back to health? Health is a conscious decision and an unhealthy life is a reflection of someone needing a nursemaid.

Depression is a mental problem, and getting older is natural. If someone makes u feel good about yourself, he's good to keep around. We gain strength from venting. It's our tool for connecting all the dots together for a more sane life.

When we vent, it helps to relieve pressure and stress. We will feel and look great! Even our mind gets on board of thinking good thoughts. We connect with our spiritual part of us, the glue that holds us together. Get healthy! Eat things that r good for u not against u! Get Healed! Be happier! Get relaxed! Get out of bad relationships! It's not easy conquering giants in our lives and a relationship can be a big problem. What about your health? He's not worth gaining a hundred pounds over. Don't sell your soul? It won't be worth it at the end. Think of ways to turn yourself into a happier healthier u. Think of ways to relax. This is a form of exercising the body mind and spirit.

*Y should we go through the process of revealing
ourselves to our potential mate.
After all he/she is a potential mate and might just
spill our secrets to the enemy his next real mate.*

CHAPTER 13
Body Odor

One big list

Hey, you stink. I mean hey, you really stink.

"I really do want to tell him he has body odor," says Kaley.

"Well if u can live with the funk, don't,tell him" laughed Gia.

"I don't understand why he won't take a shower or at least wash, and I'm too embarrassed to tell him. He's tall and cute. When we first met, I thought he was the perfect guy for me," Kaley said.

"Kaley, you have been seeing him for two months now, and I think it's time you say something to him," Gia said.

"I know, but I just don't know how," Kaley said.

Hey the guy is cute. The guy has a winning smile and great personality that you like. It's hard to resist those warm eyes of his. Fun time is over and now it's time to say, you need to take a shower. While ur in there, brush your teeth. If he doesn't wash, he doesn't care about his personal hygiene.

———

Body odor is no laughing matter. Good practice is practical. There r always two sides of the coin. The love of your life might just have medical problems and probably needs to go c a doctor.

There is a gentler way of telling someone to brush their teeth or that they have body odor. Be kind when u approach the person. If that person is a friend, you can easily start the conversation out with offering a mint. Still, this is touchy, the person could be thinking:

"What u trying to say, my breath stinks?"

I know this sucks, because sometimes u have already popped a mint into ur mouth and then someone offers u another one. Sometimes, you are chewing gum your friend offers you a stick and already sees you chewing. I don't know what this implies, but it has happened to me. I say to myself don't they see me chewing already. It can be embarrassing, but the gentler approach works better, because u don't want to offend the person. Keep this on your list 4 ever. Is it polite or is it right?

No one likes bad breath. Bad breath can come from poor health or the food we're eating. When ur on a date take those Listerine packets with you to rinse your mouth out. It's easy to slip one on your tongue. It's easy rinsing your mouth out when you ask to use the washroom. It's easy to use and by the way, I find it easier and less embarrassing by using one in front of someone and they will get the picture. Sometimes when you offer someone might be thinking you're saying they have bad breath. We don't want to admit these things, but it's harmless when you show them in a proper manner.

Friends can joke about it and get away with

hurting a persons feeling, but you don't want to do it without someone u don't know or are dating. If two months to a year have passed anything goes.

Taking care of your body is the far most important thing for both young men and women. Yet, many girls who haven't had training in these areas are just as bad as the guys. Some girls don't get trained until they are in college, and they r trained by roommates. Yeah, when they are roommates, sometimes the roommate has to school them on a few things even the facts of life.

Don't blame them because maybe they don't know anything about douching or washing after sex, especially if they're still virgins.

If they do they are too afraid to walk into a store and buy the things to keep them clean. Hey, STDs are still around! Sure, the school teaches safe sex and about ur body, but 4 the most part these girls are still insecure and walking in the store to buy these feminine products. The mind movie just happens to play out the dramatic scene of thinking what the cashier is thinking especially if she's an older man or woman. It's the waiting game - seeing who's looking as u r looking behind u hoping that no one is coming.

Then, there is the waiting for the line to get empty. Then, there is always the nosy way of finding out is going through ur roommate's things when she's not there or sometimes glancing over at them every now and then to see what they are using.

Next, is the conversation that seems un-cool, by risking the embarrassment that, "I just don't know." If I asked my mother she would flip out and want to know why and think it's bonding time."

She will be on the defensive seeing the innocent drip from her daughter's face and the innocent smile she once knew that now is scaring the heck out of her.

Girls and body Odor:
Simple solution for girls 18 and older:
If you have never been trained don't blame your mother. Don't put the blame on anyone because there is too much information out here that will cause you to have a brain freeze over all the possibilities.

Taking care of your body isn't hard to find. If you have a computer, look it up on line. If you just can't face the facts ask someone. Don't be embarrassed to ask questions. Moms get embarrassed, especially when talking about sex and taking care of your body. It's an obligation. They owe it to you to take care of these things before you leave for college or on your own.

A simple guide on how to wash the right way
You might just be saying, "I know how to wash." Yeah we all do but do we do it in the right way. The proper way is to wash below without risking infection.

First: You wash your face first, arms, chest, stomach without touching your pubic hairs or vaginal area. Then your thighs outer parts not enter.

Secondly: You wash under arms. Use another towel for washing pubic hairs and vagina. Use a scrub towel for soapy results. Never and I mean never wash between the buns first and then your vagina. You must wash your vagina first and after you are done risk the towel twice if you do not have an extra towel to use, and put soap on the towel and start all over again between the buns. If you want to do the buns first do not wash the vagina. Never wash your face with the same towel you wash between ur buns and vagina. If you are washing both areas at the same time you are at risk for vaginal infections.

Douching is easy just follow the instruction, but make sure that u get a douche that is right for u because some scented kind causes irritation. If you're not having sex, you really don't need to douche.

Some medical experts don't believe a woman should douche at all, but you can check with a doctor or call and ask a nurse. Call a doctor's office, they will be more than happy to offer you free advice, and you don't even have to tell them your name. If your body is holding an odor no matter how many time you shower or bath call to make an appointment with your doctor as I stated before it could be a medical reason.

Planning an intimate Dinner Party

Now, this is not your old fashioned mom's dinner party. You can step it up a bit by adding your book club or a few good friends. There r always dos and don'ts to having people over that you might not want to see. Of course, by invitation only will exclude the loud and obnoxious people and troublemakers. The idea is that you r tired of interruptions when you go out to dinner or being with people that make you feel uncomfortable. If you have never given a dinner party then start with some-thing nice and simple. If you don't know how to get started, consultant a dinner party planner or look on line for the simplest way to do it. Don't be ashamed to ask a friend, relative to help u prepare a dish. If you don't have a theme, ask a person who knows how to decorate for the occasion.

Etiquette

Never assume everybody likes what you like. When u invite a person over 4 dinners do u ever asked them what they might like to eat? We quickly assume that everybody eats fish or whatever we like. This is not the case. A lot of people have allergies. Then, u don't want to force them to eat something you fixed. They might try it just because you went through a lot of trouble of preparing a dinner and inviting you over.

Get the list straight before disaster happens. Plan ahead before you go shopping. While you are sitting down talking on your first date, you might want to ask the person if they allergic to any food and what they like and what they don't like.

You don't necessarily have to sit there and take out a pen and notepad. Take mental notes as you are talking about food. Cook something easy. Don't try to impress if you haven't tried it on anyone else, but yourself. I think trying to impress is highly overrated, yet we still want to feel some what validated by others. Don't spend hours in a kitchen, so if the date goes wrong you won't feel so guilty.

Ask mom to help you cook your first meal if you aren't such a great cook. Dinner and a movie are followed by the third date rule - sex. Really? It doesn't have to b this way. Afterward your guest will compliment you on what a great cook and host you are. You will smile and feel that you deserve the compliments, (after all you the one that planned it and wanted it to be a success) and you will feel good about yourself, because it was a success. Your friends will rave about for months to come. After dinner, makes sure you plan small talk before introducing a board game. Scramble is very nice, because you will see how smart the guy you want to date is. It's funny and it's not intimidating. You can tell if he's competitive or not and if he gets upset over the smallest things. It's a way of testing your dinner guest, the cute guy you invited into your home and hopefully your heart.

Sport Lovers: If you don't like sports, tell your friend, "Hey, I just don't like sports!" If he loves the games at least he'll know not to watch it around you. I had introduced a friend to a really nice guy that I've known for years. He had never been married and she had just come out of a bad married three years prior. She had a lot of trust issues and wanted to meet a nice guy. They ended up dating and falling in love. He was a good provider and he enjoyed his sports. She loved everything about him, but not the part about watching sports. After five years into the marriage, she wanted a divorce over something as trivial as sports. Her first marriage ended after her husband had an affair. She wanted to talk to me, and I didn't see a huge problem, but she did.

"He watches sports all the time," she snaps at me.

"You knew the man loved sports when you met him," I replied.

"I didn't know how much," she snapped again.

"You dated the man for two years surely you could see the signs of him watching sports. "You have it so good. Some women would rather put up with the sports issue and you're just complaining. Then, I asked her, how's everything going on with you ex-husband?"

"He's fine. Why did you ask?

"Because the last time you told me that they were having problems before they got married, and you saw it as a chance to work out your problems with him. You two started seeing each other and he was winding and dining you up until he solved his issues with the other woman. He ended up marrying the woman. I just don't want to see you make that same mistake over again. I don't want you to leave this wonderful guy I introduced to you."

Maybe this is a question I should have never asked, because she was rather vague about it.

After this confrontation she never called again. When I call her, she acts like she doesn't want to talk to me. I went over to her house and left her a card for her birthday along with some notes. Now when I call her number, it has been changed. I really think something else is going on with her.

Avoid sports fanatics! If he thinks sports, he eats sports! He sleeps sports! If he must see every game, chances are he is a sports fanatic. If he paints his body, even at home, watch out. If u have a dog or cat, he might just end up painting them too! If you know he is this way before you get serious you might not want to think about going any further and end it now unless you can live with it.

Wanted: Young Man, Single, and Free Need Not Apply Issues:

Looking for Superman/Superwoman is really what u r looking for in a relationship? Where is the so-called superman? Is he still around? Look, it's a bird it's a plane, no it's plane Jane looking for a guy who's not looking for her. No superheroes need to apply to my list. No high school dropouts, jailbirds, or who once flew over the coo...coos...nest, no relying on his parents' money. He may not be living at home with a good cause.

The good cause is he's finished with college, and he lost his job, and got kicked out of his apartment. (Reason only he can explain, but still not good enough for us.) He lost his job over foolishness. He thinks getting high is living the good life! Lazy and unreliable and sleep all day. She doesn't keep the house clean and you are stumbling over trash and a sink of dirty dishes! Nothing to eat when he gets home from a hard day of work! The daily task is trying to leap over all these tall piled up in a single bound everyday, bills, problems, and a truck load of necessaries that pushes people over the edge.

The superman and the superwoman never learned to save their money. They're too busy spending and never saving for tomorrow and now they want to blame it on everybody except the blamers - themselves. They are living the dream, and never wanting to wake up to reality.

Yet, she has found love with her so called superman, and his so called super woman. The sexy Lois Lane with long legs and sexy body that won't quit up until the aging process begins. The superman starts looking for another superwoman to quickly take her place, because she has become overweigh or ghostly.

When Lois Lane isn't getting the attention she deserves, she turns to chocolate donuts and bon bons. (See chapter on exercise and chocolate) She then turns their 3.4 children against the man she once loved. He tries to redeem himself, but she won't let him? He's sexy and playful. He is the high definition of sexiest man of the year and he looks and smells the part. He doesn't want to make love to his overweight superwoman and living happily ever after seems so far away. Like most super heroes the superman abuses his super powers and they both become something they don't recognize any more. He never recognizes that she was once his everything.

What do u believe in?

I've never seen so many people fight over religion, but it is the most important thing in a relationship. (Check out the next chapter, The Girlfriend's List, for more juicy details) What do u believe in? If you can't get it together, don't date and certainly don't marry. Sooner or later, this subject will come up again and can brew into a heated argument. It's like burning the American Flag! I mean when the flag is up, don't bring it down to the ground and step all over it or set it on fire. The same goes for your personal beliefs. If you can find a common ground where u both are comfortable without the heated decision, then maybe your relationship stands a chance. I don't care how cute the guy is. I don't care how cute she is. If you can't compromise leave it alone. In fact, leave each other alone.

Finding the opposite sex:

Ladies, if you can't get it through your head you might want to have your head examined again. We have already narrowed it down. I know we want the romance; the forever after wedding. (See Royal)

A twenty-year-old man isn't ready to settle down or even gets into a serious relationship. If nobody told you, well there it is! If it seems like sex is all they want, well they do. So don't go calling his mother on the phone and saying, "He's a dog!" (See Chapter on Clarification of Dogs and Pigs) They have been waiting for it for so long when they couldn't get it in their teen years. It drives them crazy when they first taste the honey, and they're driven to sexual desires. Eventually, they will be looking for that good girl who doesn't sleep around. It will be on their terms not yours, and when he finds her he will make the ultimate commitment - marriage. If he's a lot older than twenty something, then u know he might just b looking 4 a mate. The question is r u approachable? Or do you carry the scarlet letter across your forehead? It's simple math B + A =Bad Attitude.

Where u might find him or her: He could be looking 4 u in the Laundromat. He's single and he has to do his own laundry. When men shop, they r looking for something specific. Just shop and linger 4 ever. A man could be shopping in a sense, but at the same time, looking for a mate. If he happens to ask you where to find something, chances r he thinks u r approachable and attractive. At a gas station: He just might be talking about the price of gas and smile at you and hoping you will reply. You might also find him at a wedding/reception. He will be asking who's single. (Don't appear stuck up)

At the library (Yeah, they hang out there all the time) He might want to accidentally bump into u if you catch his eye.

You might also find the ideal guy walking or working in your yard as he is taking a walk.

The right man might be at the bakery (Y a bakery? Women r always buying sweets, are planning birthday parties, weddings, baby showers, or engagement parties. The reason u don't notice the men is because ur 2 busy purchasing ur order. U don't remember bumping into that cute guy and you only exchange smiles. Remember Sleepless in Settle? What a memorable movie! I watch it over and over again. It's amazing, because I can remember meeting a guy just like that except I wasn't at an airport. I never saw him again. You will do the same, always wondering what ever happened to that guy that bumped into you.

Radio Station. He might just call the station while u r doing the interview, and ask the questions, "Who was that woman? Is she nice looking?" Who knows the owner just might give him a message. He might be the guy in the audience and call the show.

Other places where you could find nice guys:
- Side walk café'
- Beach
- Restaurant (He just might c u eating along and trying 2 c if u r approachable.
- Dinner party (He might be invited to a dinner party by a friend)

- Jogging or walking (He might c u walking ur dog and express dearly that he luv animals.) Not like Boomer Rang with earn two stars and should have earned more by the critics but then what do they know.
- On Campus   Football game/Basket ball game/baseball game
- He might b in uniform (Women haven't changed that much they still love a guy in uniform.)

Harsh words are worse than a slap across the face. Both can have an impact that will affect u for the rest of ur life. Get out! Get Free! Seek forgiveness! Seek peace!

CHAPTER 14
Reflection/Blame

When I began to write the female list I was sure it was going to be longer than the male's list, but not so. The females lists were rather short whereas the male's were rather long. Most guys don't want a woman who will mess around. Reflection: Say it with me, "Most men become very threaten when their women sleep with someone else. They can't handle it well. They r not so forgiving. Yes, they did add in*fidelity* to their list. Of course, we know that women act like they r so hard up 4 a man when really, they just have to 4 give the ones they have and work it out.

Maybe it's some kind of secret competition they also feel threaten that they r not good enough and being rejected as a child, teenager and now as an adult and they don't like the way that feel. Or maybe it's the blue print of the woman and the foundation on which she was made. Don't blame her she didn't make herself. We must remember that we can easily become enablers of abuse and alcoholic. Yet, I was very surprise what this young woman had to say, and I did mix it in what the 38 and beyond said as well.

Men have fought wars over women and religion. The big do's and don'ts, the will's and won'ts. It's not negotiable! As one person put it, "Frankly, honey, I don't give a... what u believes." I really wasn't surprised this is how people perceive the world they live in. This is how they perceive their evils and goods. This may surprise u, because I know, but if you want don't want to have a fiery argument that may result in the death of any relationship including marriage, never debate about religion or your beliefs.

Religion and politics cause the number one arguments between the sexes. They almost top the list over cheating and money. If u really love this girl/guy, u should probably not even consider dating or marriage if you have religious differences. You can end up fighting the whole time. What I mean by fighting is arguing about who's right and who's wrong.

No matter how cute the girl/guy is you have to make a good, sound decision. If you think it won't come up again because u have conquered it, think again. People have gone to war of this very same thing "Together we stand. Divided we fall." In this case love doesn't conquer all. Y would u put yourself through the torment of raising children and forcing them to choose sides? Y put yourself through your mate's visiting my church every blue moon.

Count down on the girlfriend's list/What the girls have to say about their order of things.
1.Love

2. Respect (yourself first and then others)

3. Honesty (Don't lie or embellish who u r)

4. Trust

5. Self Reliance

6. Priorities

7.Temperance (especially in public places, restaurant, (See the chapter on restaurant behavior) getting groceries, shopping at the mall. I can't stress this enough. Most men don't like shopping and rather be with their friends. Of course, they don't want to hurt your feelings especially when you're trying to get to know each other. Now, here's a new thought - Go shopping as a couple. He can hang with his guy friend while u have ur friend. He wants to be included in shopping, just not with you. But, like I said before, he will fake it all the way to make u think he's really enjoying himself. To make us happy he will fake it all the way home.)

8. Good personal hygiene

9. Strength

10. Sensibility

11. Doesn't have 2 b out going if I'm not (home body need not to apply)

12. No mama's boy

13. No drugs (Don't even look my way)

14. Don't overly drinks (if I don't drink I don't want a man who drinks.)

15. Party too much

16. I don't want a guy who doesn't want to grow up

17. Practical, handy

18. Handles rejection well

19. Good attitude not explosive

20. Puts family first (If we decide to get married, I want to know if I will come first (before anyone)

even his mother.

21. Must be interesting, not boring

22. Responsible

23. No uninteresting guys

24. Attractive enough to take outside. I don't want a man who doesn't care about his appearance not even on those off days.

25. Eats properly at nice restaurants and yes, will pick up the bill unless we agree to go Dutch.

26. I don't want a guy who acts like a girl, but still have his masculinity in tact. People might think I'm gay or crossing over to dating guys with feminine attributes.

27. A guy who dresses well, but not as good as I do or think he looks as good as I do

29. A gentlemen without over doing it.

30. A guy that my friends like, because I might just want to have friends over and it's very uncomfortable when no one likes the guy ur dating.

31. I admire a guy who can handle himself in the kitchen, but not overtake over my duties. It would be nice to come home to a home cooked meal if I'm working late or tired.

32. Never flamboyant.

34. Must speak well enough to be understood and does not run his sentences together.

35. An accent is okay.

Male List
  1. Sexual gratification
  2. Companionship
  3. Warm meals
  4. No drama queens

5. Live by intellect and not by feelings (Have to be able to solve problem without flying off the handle.) (Clear thinking comes up with correct mood or words 4 any occasion.

6. Love $ Respect (Giving and receiving respect)

7. Mature commitment (Good 4 both family unit to be as successful as you can be.

8. Avoiding (I don't want my house or apartment rearranged apartment because I'll feel obligated to u. This way I can avoid obligation.)

9. I want date a boyish type woman. She can like sports, but come on I don't want her hanging around guy friends like that. It's competition in all things that men do and women become like a sport.

10. Man cave. (Should be left alone. If not, it will become a woman's cave. I don't want my woman turning my man cave into some girly girl type of setting.)

11. Steady movement (better n relationship)

"More sex and more sex (her appetite must meet mine. She must enjoy making love as much as I do.) If she doesn't well that can be a problem. Most women will fake it, and that's wrong to a man. Then, we end up marrying these women and they trap u that way, and then later say, "I don't like to make love. I don't feel like it." I don't like it when women fake it. They think guys can't tell. Well, we can, especially when you start growling like some animal when a man wants to make love. It makes me wonder if that is why I saw my dad with dirty magazines under his mattress."

12. Self preservation (Don't call me I'll call u.) When I'm ready I will call. Until then, I consider it bugging me or getting too close when I said I like u and not love u... Or I say I want to take u out on a date, and not to put a ring on your finger. I think all dates should be explained to women.

13. Truthful (direct not trickery.
    No double deal (lie how u r inside)
    I don't want to settle second best. (What the next best thing to a perfect relationship, because a little bit of happiness is worth more than all of none.

14. I don't want a girl who has had more than three boyfriends. I don't want a girl that sleeps around with just anybody. If I wanted to date an all around the town girl, I would do so, but I don't want that.

"I want a girl to take home and introduce to my mother.

15. Inner Beauty, she must know herself first before she gives herself to me. I've been through the pain of the ex-boyfriend drama. She still had feelings for the guy. He did her wrong and I didn't know if she really was over him or if I should end the relationship. I don't like to be fooled. If u r still seeing ur old boyfriend, then we need 2 talk. Your mess isn't worth losing my mind over. Your mess isn't worth ruining me. That's not easy 4 a guy to admit, but it really gets serious." If I'm true blue, then I want her to be the same.

16. infidelity (Don't c anybody else but me. No

bizarre women.) I want a woman who behaves well in public. If she's yelling at her kids or hitting them on side of the head in public she's not the kind of woman I want to date. They always say that u can tell how good a man is by how he treats his mother. Well, I feel if a woman doesn't treat her mother with respect I don't want to be bothered with her. It doesn't matter to me if they haven't resolved some issue. It makes me wonder what kind of woman/wife/mother she would be to our future children. I run from women with a bad attitude. I don't want a bossy woman in no shape or form, and I don't care if she has a killer body.

17. Illusive perfunctory
18 Mean and nasty
19. Pouty and powerless
20. Lazy
21. A girl who can enjoy different

Wrong Signal? Turn Right
Leads to open exposure

Two Guys Stories:

Touchy is as Touchy Does

I was really curious about the attitude of one young man, who appeared to have no particular interest in the female hanging on his shoulder. I was interested in what he thought about dating girls that are not his age. I never brought up his taste in women, and his choice of geeky clothes that somehow complimented his short, spiked haircut.

He blasted it out there like I was asking him

about the cute, dark complexion Asian American girl wrapped around his neck like the bright checker scarf she was wearing with her sports jacket. This was clearly a guy who had made his mind up and was fed up with some American women. Yet, he remains positive and optimistic about dating girls that in his age category. The young man started out with some very serious word too strong even for me, so you are getting the condensed version of what he said. He really had a lot to say. His girlfriend nodded her head in agreement. I could tell she really like him.

"Hey, I'm just like any other person," says a thirty something. I don't know what to do anymore. The girl agrees to relations and then when she does, she says its rape. I would rather just not date girls like that. You see it all the time on the news and I don't want to be one of those guys. I look out for all kinds of signals. Guys r really getting into trouble. My mama didn't raise no fool. I hate it when girls lie on men and the whole world seems to believe them. Guys don't have any support system, but the girls do. He laughed, "I need to be writing my own book on the subject. You see a nice looking girl at a party, and then she has too much to drink and all of a sudden she cries rape. This happened to one of my friends when we were in high school. The dude hasn't been the same since. Far as I'm concern she ruined dude's life! I am a very cautious person.

Nowadays, they will have u all over the news without the celebrity treatment. Dudes, dating use to be fun! I mean fun! I heard these older people talk about it all the time, but for my generation it has become crazy. You've got baby mama drama...and don't even look at a younger woman. It was cool in my grandparent's days, but now days, they will put you in jail and call you a child molester 'cause you like younger women.

Even if they have a hot body, hey, I keep my distance and keep it to myself. I don't even joke about it with a friend, because that so called friend might just put what you say out there. We should get smart and tell girls to sign an agreement before we go on a date. We don't have any rights when it comes to girls. We don't have anyone to fight for us. They portray us as some pervert horny guys who want to take advantage of women. We should go back to the old days and get a chaperon or at least take another couple along with us. American girls have gotten so crazy with all the nonsense, so I mostly date foreign girls, such as Asians or middle easterners. Even the Hispanic girls r getting crazy. With all the madness, I stay away from them too, because they have become so Americanized and caught up with all the craziness.

I do want to clear up one thing - I like our women, but I can live without all of the nonsense. Most of my friends are dating Asian girls too."

Dance with Me:
"You caught me on a good day," the guy smiled.
"What is that supposed to mean to me," I said.
"This is a day I feel like talking and I just came back from a job interview and I feel pretty good right now. I know I landed that job."

The conversation started out great and I believe he gave me his honest answer on dating girls and asking them for that first dance.

"Man, you see more girls on the dance floor than you see guys dancing with them. Guys love to see it, but me I like it the old fashioned way. When a boy asks a girl to dance, girls look at us like we're some kind of freaks! But it is them that's acting like freaks, rubbing and touching each other and even kissing each other. Some guys like the lesbian girls dancing. I'm not saying they are Lesbos, but they act like them on the dance floor. These girls are so cold u really don't want 2 ask them to dance. You never see guys dancing with each other unless they are in a gay bar or club. I guess they think it turns on a guy, because they look at us as if they want us to join in. For me, I just want to throw up it's insane! I'm not saying that in a good way either. No guy likes to be shot down when they ask a girl to dance. Sometimes they can be down right mean. They tease you like they want to see your reaction to being let down. It's a waste of time.

If a girl keeps looking at you and smiling that's when it seems to be a sign to ask her to dance, but then her friend eye-balls you with contempt. I keep my hands to myself. It's all about reading the right signal from the girl. If her hands are folded, u know she doesn't want to be bothered. If she smiles and touches her hair, I believe at that point she's noticing u noticing her so it becomes okay to approach her. I don't want to get hit like my friend did. Smack! The girl went right upside his head. He couldn't do anything but stand there. He tried to redeem himself and started dancing by himself until the embarrassment wore off.

I walked up to him and asked him if he was alright. He was pissed and went to the bar and ordered a drink and left. Luckily, it wasn't a slow dance. He really would have looked foolish. You have to be careful how you approach these girls. They have cameras on their phones and record you. I don't like it when you're trying to talk to a nice girl and she's on the phone totally disrespecting you. Even after you get a date with her, she's yapping on the phone to her friends, a total turn off.

I don't call any more. When I see her number I ignore it for that reason.   I had the nerve one day to ask my mom where to meet nice girls. Man, that was a mistake. Never ask your mom where to meet girls. They are too "parentage. "

I sat there at the table one day and asked that question. My mom's face light up as if I was telling her I could solve world hunger or something like that. Moms are too judgmental. My mom and dad met at a club, but she doesn't want me looking for girls in a club. She has been married to my father for thirty-five years now.

They will swear that clubbing is no place to look for nice girls. I like the atmosphere in some clubs, but it has to be the right club and not where undesirable people hang out. The club has to have a good reputation; still I don't go all the time. Sometimes, I go where they are serving food and drinks, but I'm not that much of a drinker. If I see a girl ordering drink after drink I don't even approach her. I figure if a girl wants to dance they will ask me, and I'm cool with that. My friend and I would grab a table and we would see these girls walking in with these old farts. That's why it's hard for us to get dates because of these old farts. They have taking over and they are probably married with children."

Remember when the girl would say, "Would u respect my mind as well as my body? (Recap) Who can respect a girl/young woman's mind when u c so much sex and it's every where you go? When men react, we think they are like she dogs in heat. Just tell little Tommy to keep that thing in his pants under control. The translation is lost!"

If guys really want to know what we like, he should study us a little closer. Spontaneity always works especially when u have a fun person in your life. But hey, people change.

CHAPTER 15
Behaving ugly at a restaurant

I am drawing behaving ugly at a restaurant from my own experiences and the things I've seen. I had to add this chapter after seeing one of my daughter's favorite talk shows. She talked me into watching the show about five women sitting around talking about everything. Two of the hosts happened to be my favorite people in show biz. I don't think it would be wise to mention the name of the show. I was shock to see one of the hosts pick up a pork chop with her hand and started chewing on it as if she had not eaten for a month as the camera zoomed in on her. I don't think she knew that the cameras were on her.

Granted, she is a comedian and I like her, but I found it very ill-mannered and embarrassing. I was hoping at that moment that a child wasn't looking, because every parent would have to explain to them about manners.

I don't think she was embarrassed. Besides this I'm just glad she didn't start picking her teeth. I said to myself, "Give her a minute or two and she will be picking her teeth with her finger." I still can't believe she did this on national TV!

Restaurants are always on the biggest list of all for when people want to show out or tell u off. Who wants someone to be loud, rude, and obnoxious to the waiter? Well, I went out with friends to a restaurant while we were on our way to a function out of town. On the way there, they discussed where they wanted to eat. In the conversation, I heard them claim to be Christians and serve the most High.

In fact, all they talked about was their beliefs and what people should and should not be doing. It even got to a point where they were debating some issues; although, this in itself is debatable. I didn't care to comment so right away someone thought something was wrong.

One lady seemed to be a nice person, but she wouldn't let anyone get a word in. She was so rude, always interrupting when someone wanted to say something. I said to myself, "Here we go again - another person who thinks she knows everything."

You know the idiom – "*Two peas in a pod.*" I felt trapped between these two people. I was used to one of those ladies who always has an opinion opposed on others and thinks she's right about everything. She is very talkative, opinionated, outspoken, and sometimes doesn't consider others' feelings and always wants to control the conversation. It makes u want to tell her to shut up and let someone else get a word in. She does have some very nice qualities such as she's a caring, nice and kind person that everybody admires and loves to be around. We all have faults. Sometimes, she calls me and I'm not in the mood to talk to her because in the first three words I can tell where the conversation is going to go.

Now we're sitting at the table getting ready to order our meal. As the woman looks at the menu, she started complaining about how high the prices are. I had to make a minor adjustment and try not to offend her. I was becoming a little irritated and said to myself, "What have I gotten myself into?" I should have thought about that before I left home and followed my first mind not to go.

Sometimes it is our fault for the choices we make and sometimes they aren't all bad. I was stuck, I had to deal with my situation, and I was grateful that she asked me and grateful for our friend for paying for our meal. That's why I thought of idioms that were similar to others. One saying goes, "If u have to ask the price, u can't afford it." U r in a good place, when someone else is paying.

All I could think about at the time I was invited to come, and the gentlemen we were with was a friend of mine who happened to be in love with my friend whom I had known over twenty years. You don't have to go overboard when someone says, "I'm paying. Order what u want." It would be nice to see what they r ordering and don't try to super exceed their cost. Show them that u do have temperance in ordering your meal. Politely ask them if it's okay that u order the New York Steak if you don't want the fish. If he/she doesn't want to order dessert, then ask if it's okay for u to order dessert. Sometimes after ur dinner is over people don't want dessert and prepare to leave, so this way you can ask the waiter to bring it to you in a carry out container. Where most things are common sense 2 u, they may not b common sense to another person.

The woman who was with us kept calling the server over to our table. She was complaining about everything. At that moment I think it began to sink in, and that maybe she would let the poor guy go and do his job. When he finally left the table, she looked in our friend's plate, the one who had paid for our meal, and started complaining again. Our wonderful friend was a gentleman, and wanted to please everybody, so he offered her some of his food on his plate. I can't speak for him, but it seems that he was getting tired of her complaining as well.

Y didn't she order the same meal that we were having, rather than complaining and manipulating the situation. I just couldn't believe it! She asked me a question, and I didn't want to answer her because I didn't want to debate about the meal she had ordered.

It almost became comical to me and I could have taken advantage of the situation, but I didn't.

It did come to a point where she became very annoying, disruptive, and loud. Talk about being stuck between a rock and a hard place. Whether it's a 5 star or no star at all at least be aware of ur attitude towards the waiter or waitress. Even if it's a nice, quaint restaurant, mind ur manners. Some people come with a mind of giving the servers a hard time. People like this seem to have rehearsed what they r going to say to the servers before they arrive at the restaurant.

They r not happy with the way their own lives r so they have to give the servers a hard time. You can ask yourself a few questions. What do I want to get out of this experience while I'm sitting with friends at dinner? Premeditate: Some people r not in control over their actions. They r there to make other people suffer without blinking an eye. "Well, I'm going to make this server feel as bad as I'm feeling. She doesn't smile enough. She's not catering to my needs. She'll have to work for this tip if I decide to give her a tip at all. When I flagged her, she looks the other way. My food isn't hot enough! My food is too cold. My water isn't cold enough. I didn't get the service I was expecting, so I'm not going to leave a tip. If no one else is complaining why should u go against the grain of life? U have to make ur request known to the waiter before u send him on the mission of filling your order. Make sure you know
what u want before u order it. Make sure u let him know if you want your meat well done, medium or rare. Let him know how you like your fish, chicken or steak. Let them know that you don't want salt or butter on your baked potatoes. Ask for a substitute for butter and especially for salad dressing. If you prefer light then order light. If you don't like the side dishes, ask them if you could substitute the dish before u sink your teeth into something you find very distasteful, and your friends finds themselves dealing with your distasteful attitude. He/she is there to serve u, but u have to know that they r human too. What goes around comes around - sometimes twice.

Your server just might be putting him/herself through medical school and guess what, they just might be your doctor one day. Don't dismiss the fact that you r on vacation or just visiting on the other side of town and eating out. Even if you r in another state, the young server could be transferred to your state and just happen to be your doctor at the hospital where you might be a patient. Imagine that this same person coming to your town to work as a teacher who will be teaching you or your child, a judge in a courtroom and has to hear your case! Now that's something to think about! Careful how u treat people, especially strangers! Yeah, I took it that far!

Out with friends:

It's crazy when u r out with friends and you know what to expect from them, but then when they bring an outsider along you might be asking for trouble. I have been in this situation too many times and now I have given up on the idea of going out with friends when they invite a new person. I would like to set up a casual meeting with these outside friends. Yeah, y not let me c what they r like before you toss the idea of going out to dinner with them. Some people love drama! Some people r jealous that u came along and they r going to try to do everything that they can to make u feel uncomfortable.

If u r already in the company of your outspoken, opinionated friend, but are used to it and don't mind the drama from them y should u put yourself through the drama of someone new? It's not that serious!

The next time you're out with your male/female friend, ask yourself, "R they worthy of eating out at a nice restaurant?"

The list goes like this: If u want to go, then

prepare yourself to be the wise one and say as little as possible and avoid subjects that you don't care to discuss such as religion and politics, especially with people who already think they know everything and like to either debate or argue.

My review: The Queen of Kings Carrie syndrome at a restaurant scene:

I really like watching this sitcom, even the reruns since the show has been cancelled. In one scenario, Doug likes the restaurant and he wants a place he and his wife could go and call their own. I thought that was so cute. Who doesn't want to go to a place where everybody knows your name? Kerrie doesn't want to go out and wants to stay home, but Doug is so excited that he has found this great restaurant. Carrie Usually rejects every good idea Doug has and this was one of them. Carrie gets upset because she feels that the waiter has shunned her. Carrie complains, but the root of her problems extends from the fact that she didn't want to go to the restaurant. She always has to be in control and right about everything. Most of the time, Doug gives up and retires the idea because he wants to be happy. Carrie makes Doug feel guilty and tells him he's not going to ever eat there again and that she forbids it. Of course poor Doug caves.

Later, Carrie finds out that she is overreacting after hearing her father complain over the phone to a company from which he was buying a product. She admits she was wrong and goes back and apologize to the owner, waiter, and Doug.

How many times do we apologize to anybody especially waiters? How many times do we say we're sorry to people when we offend even if they weren't a part of the argument, but in the company of those who argue with us? How many times to do we apologize for starting trouble when it was peaceful before you came on the scene?

Dating:

U r on a date it's okay to talk about your likes and dislikes. In other words, "I hope u r not going to turn into your evil twin when we get there." Get to the root of what's bothering you before u arrive. Get it straight! Get it under control or choose not to go at all.

Or just say, "I'm eating and I'm trying to enjoy myself." If they r the ones driving, try to find another way there and meet them at the restaurant in case u want to make a quick exit. Take a cab. Drive yourself. If you go out of town, make sure you r going to be comfortable with the people u r going out of town with, because you can't easily escape. U could chalk it up with lesson learned and never go with them again. If u r not feeling it, don't go. Remember, it was u that put yourself in that situation in the first place. U have no one to blame but yourself. Next time, listen to that little voice in your head.

Inviting the A list:

If you're dining in, make sure u tell your friends it is not a house party and you're only inviting a selective group of people. The friends you invite should get your permission to bring other with them. "I was so excited when I was invited to Ms. Peggy's Forrester's house. I bumped into her a store, and we started talking. I wasn't invited over her house when she gave her intimate dinner parties and never felt left out because she didn't invite me. Her circle of friends included people who own businesses, the rich and not famous. Everybody knows that she was the most wonderful person to be around. I guess u can say if you live in a small city the Mayor seems famous as well as the city councilman and lawyers. When I saw her, she was all smiles as usual and told me about her day as she played catch up with me. We never even talked on the phone, but when we saw each other it was like we kept in touch all the time. On this particular day, she was so excited about her New Year's breakfast. Of course I accepted an invitation from her without hesitation.

"Would you like to come to my New Year's breakfast?" she asked me.

"Really?" I asked smiling.

"Yes, I want you to come and you can bring someone with you," she said.

Right away, I knew who I was going to ask. Our small city was only twenty miles from her beautiful home, and I loved driving that way on weekends.

"Yes, I really want u to come," she smiled warmly.

"Sure," she replied. "I'm making my list so I'll know how much to serve. Give me your information again and I'll send the invitation out in the mail. If you won't be attending, please call me and let me know."

I gave her the information she asked for, and did as she asked. You see, when u r invited, let the person who is inviting you talk and state what they want from u, and if you can bring someone else along. I was happy because I was always apart of the Mayngil (May never get invited list) list. This is what I call the Never list. If you get on the "A" list, people think ur worthy. If you're on the "B" list you get invited often enough, but when ur on the "C" list, you only get invited on occasion.

When it goes all the way down you're the one who's always look
ed over or left out. Sometimes the social scene can be important, but I wouldn't stress over it if you're never invited.

Jealousy/Envy:
Jealousy is so ugly. These people don't belong to us. Their expiration date might end at any time while u r dating them. Don't put demands on friendships or relationships. Most men get jealous of women who have a male friend even if they knew them since they were kids, grade school or high school even in college, church, or on a job. Yet, their friendship grew and they have never had any romantic involvement. There are some male and females who are friends who have never had a
sexual relationship EVER! Most men will think u r interfering with their heads and I'm not taking about the ones on their shoulders; although, you might think that they r one in the same.

Women r the same way. They have a need to know if a guy has ever been romantically involved with the other female. They want to know why she hangs around so much. Y does she always call on u when she has a problem? U will have a problem when it comes to marrying the woman and she doesn't understand ur friendship. She thinks you should be friends only with her friends. This is a disaster from the start. No one wins!

We need to come to the conclusion that we are two individuals and that we grew up in separate or maybe in the same area or neighborhoods. We went to the same school or different schools. We went to the same church or different churches or maybe did not have any kind of religious opportunity at all. Either way, we met and fell in love.

He has friends and you have friends and had them before you met him/her. Get over the fact that he/she might have a friend who happens to be the opposite sex. If there were more than friendship, it's time to share so you won't run the other person crazy. He/she won't be tormented because you have a sexier friend than you r. If there wasn't anything going on, share it and be honest with your partner to be.

Guys keep secrets:

This is a little known fact. Guys r not comfortable talking about sex or about themselves with women. Guys r not comfortable talking about old girlfriends. Some r not comfortable talking about a friend who happens to be a girl, but will share if it will keep their partners from asking questions. Don't be surprised when they don't want to talk about having a girl for a friend and often times they don't have anything to hide.

The woman's mind works like this - We always think that they have something to hide if they don't want to share. Speaking of sharing, it's mostly for women and not men, so you might want to go back to the question of satisfying her need to share moment. Of course, she will appear to be a lot calmer and at peace with herself. Men, what do you want? Peace or to live with a nightmare? You should be able to keep your friends and your relationship. Make sure ur friends understand the person you are in love with does come first, especially if you are married.

The Lists of all lists: Communication

A friend is a friend, but if you're having sex with that friend it becomes something more than a friendship. As the slogan goes: *Friends don't let friends drive drunk.* A man I knew told me that he had a friend, and now he's separated from his wife. "Did you sleep with her," I asked him.
"Yes," he said.
"Well, she's not a friend, you don't sleep with friend. When u slept with her she became something else to you, and now you're separated because of it. Friends don't sleep with friends."

We have 2 come 2 the understanding that a man/woman has probably had sex before they marry either with each other or someone else. Sometimes it can be meaningless and a one-night stand, but it has happened. U shouldn't get upset because your friends run into an old flame...the desire might still be there, but clearly she/he is in love with you now and won't dare cross that path again. A relationship takes work for it to last long.

TOP OF THE LIST: Nvr b little the one u love
"U won't let me b the man."

What gets us is that we do want men to validate us in some way. Let it be known to the world, I'm your girl. Let it b known to your friends I deserve respect! You're broke and I pay the bills and you don't have a job, and I brought the car, so what I say goes, and you better tell all your friends!

Listen men, we r thrown into some crazy situations today. Women r more aggressive than they ever been before. Still, that small thing called validation is needed just to smooth things over for the night. You would think that we r spoiled little girls who need some attention. When it gets crazy just duck in and duck out! The turn around is when we use to say, "You're the man." Now the guy is saying, "You're the woman." "You got it! You're paying all the bills, and won't even think about my role in all of this. You still let me not the man."

So, where r all the tears in this? The woman is no longer crying and we have turned the strong man into a sappy wimp! Well, we wanted him 2 get in touch with his feminine side, didn't we? Don't b surprised while u r bringing home the bacon, he's trying on ur underwear and shoes and sitting on the sofa eating bon bons and chocolates. When u get home, he's asking you if he could he do your hair and your nails and his small talks consist of what is happening on the soaps. You just might think he wants to become a hairdresser. Yeah right! Now you've really got a problem, you want to break up with him because now you think he's gay. Wasn't it you telling him to get in touch with his feminine side, and that you're the wo'men! Now it's too much of a good thing you're running scare.

I don't want a man looking in my closet he just might want to try on my shoes and say, "they fit!"

Fashion police says:

I am no fashion police, but I do know by watching a lot of talk shows that all of them agree on this fashion statement. The little black dress...you can't go wrong! I talked with three young women, most of them like it when guys dress up.

"My man need to know how to dress" I love a man who dresses really nice," said Keria.

"I can tell by the way he dresses he has a job and that he cares about himself," Serena says.

"A man doesn't have to dress up for me. I like casual. If he's attractive I'll take him in rags, as long as he's a man!" Even when I see him at the supermarket, " Alana says.

If u don't have these clothing items then you should make your way to the mall or department store and get them. If you don't have the money, cut out your spa, getting your nails done, or other activities lilke frying and dying your hair done so much. Stop buying that cake you've just got to have and invest in the little black dress.

You can even invest in the man that you're dating or about to date. When you date him walk through in his closet, and you'll see what he wears. Ask first, because you don't want to get your feelings hurt by rumbling through his closet. After all, you don't want him snooping around your dresser drawer or closet.

A man should have at least one nice dress coat, and it depends on what state u live in, most definitely, a nice coat, prefer black or tan: one nice suit, pair of dress slacks and a casual jacket and also one nice pair of dress shoes.

Every woman on the planet needs to invest in "the little black dress." This is a fashion must and a plus for some because it draws attention with the right accessories. The little black dress is always mistaken as a fashion statement. Despite the belly fat and problems with being overweight, the little black dress hides imperfections with a jacket, belt, wrap, and colorful scarf. A splash of color these days is in like the wind on a windy day. The breeze will just captivate you into thinking yeah; I need some color with that.

You know what nobody really matches colors any more. Well, those who are still stuck in time and behind want colors that match everything - even their accessories. The future generation who knows what off brand things of color to decide upon wearing.

Fashion changes all the time and color with it. Colored shoes don't necessarily mean it has to match your purse or clothes you're wearing. A nice pair of shoes that would go with anything you wear is good! You can never go wrong with these clothing items.

Don't dress the way you feel! This is a big no-go situation. You don't want to dress like something that the cat dragged in from the night before do you? The little black dress doesn't have to cost an arm or leg. When u invests in it you will see why you did in the first place. If you love purses make sure you get one for all seasons.

Tips on getaways:

There r so many wonderful getaways that can take u from the north, south, east and west. If you love woodland, nature, trails you can go online and seek out your pleasure island, nice restaurant, and resorts. It doesn't matter if you love the city or country atmosphere GO get away for a while, and stop talking about it. Experience a brand new u without the comparing to other places you visit. If you r going just to compare then u r going for the wrong reason! Just go to see how beautiful American really is and can b 4 u. Even if it's 50 to a 100 miles from where you live! Go west young man! Yeah, go west; a place that we often neglect with is filled with beauty.

They say its God's Country, and believe me once you go west you will see why. These are inexpensive trips! Check with your travel agency and magazines for the perfect get away. Look through travel magazine and then find out who's giving tours across the country. Call a friend, loved one, hubby, friend male or female, cousin of someone who really loves u 4 being u. You can take the journey alone with a bunch of other strangers seeking out enjoyment of meeting others on tours. This way you can get out of your comfort zone and really experience something new and think clearly about your life.

Ur mind will be clear and u will feel so great about life! U will see for urself random act of kindness. People are trying to get back to giving and loving each other without fear, so be one of them and let them without being so afraid of your own shadow.

Three years ago I met a woman on a cruise and she had just lost her husband. Her daughter treated her to a cruise because she saw that her mother needed it. Her daughter had accepted a job in Utah, and she had moved from Virginia. Her daughter loved it out there, and wanted to do something special for her mom whom she could no longer run across town to see. I could tell she still missed her husband whom she lost from an illness.

I was going to a rough time and it was one of the reasons I accept the invitation to go on the cruise. Yeah, true story. We just hit it off like we had known each other all our lives. We still keep in touch and she invited me to her wedding. She was ten years older than I was, but it works and I really enjoy being her friend.

Unlike the song on the old sitcom Cheers, "Sometimes you don't want to go where everybody knows your name." Just when you think ur the only one who wants to leave the planet, you'll find a thousand other people are right behind you.

You'll know when u really love someone when it through thick and thin and believe when the thick wear out it get thinner and thinner. When u think there is nothing else, now that's when the real test comes.

The reality of dating when it comes to your pet or pest: Pet Lover and Game Play offs

Before u even date a guy/girl you should ask them, "do you own any pets." You could be allergic or just don't like pets of any kind. You're not a dog lover. You're not a cat lover! All of that can bring trouble to paradise that would otherwise be a great love affair. Well ur boyfriend can become a pest if he doesn't love your pet. A guy who loves pets and has them and u don't can present problems for ur relationship.

You adore him, but he hates that you have a cat or dog. Either tell him or dish him. Believe me he's not going to give up his pet for u, and neither will he give up game day for u. If guys are reading this: If the girl won't give up her dog for you she's might be thinking you just might turn out to be a real dog the kind that walks on two legs.

Game Day:
Y would u give him the blues because u don't like football or any sport? Most men do and you r not the only one who has had this point of view! I say let him retrieve to his man cave and watch the game without u, because clearly you're not a fan. It was a time when game day was just for the boys when they would get together and watch the game at home or over a friend's house. This was a great opportunity to not only for them to bond with their friends but also to get a way from the women. Women felt powerless, because the man had something he could enjoy instead of her. Y not? She had her social groups, so was this too much to ask? Apparently yes. Game day means he can go out with the guys and your puppy dog eyes won't even change his mind. Clearly it's man vs. woman when
game day sets in, so I guess that's why women have joined in on the fun and learned all they could about football, basket ball, hockey, and some other manly sports.

It wasn't about socializing, because women are calling the shots before the guys get a chance 2. This is another way to enter into his man cave even if he doesn't want u there. Women learned to once again interferer like in the Garden of Eden. If Eve hadn't interfered with the divine plan, things could have been happier for us all. Yet, Adam says the divine present was that woman.

Now they will never admit that they don't want u there and sometimes when they just want to b with the guys they get up nerves to say it out loud when they have been holding it inside 4 so long. We r like that, because we want 2 b apart of him, so much we will wear his pants and take on his attitude.

A proven fact: Amelia Bloomer, fought that war, women wearing pants vs men, and their attitudes. She designed and wore them and took on their attitudes proving "these are the signs of the time." She even protested and wrote about women rights to divorce their drunken, abusive husband in 1851. They shook the world when they protested about high prices of bread in Paris on Oct 5, 1789. U c there is nothing new under the sun, someone had to started, the fire!

BREAKING IT DOWN: The complexity of a woman

What really can scare a man is this - he will never know about the complexity of a woman's mind or body. What scares a woman is they will never know the mind of a man. You might say then, how could I write about a man and what he thinks, well, I said it before I talked and interviewed them. Of course I don't what they are really thinking unless they are honest enough to tell me.

Yet, there is help if he would like to take some classes or go online to ask a simple question about females and the way they work.

The anatomy of a woman:
If you are really desperate, ask ur mother or grandmother and they may not understand everything about themselves because women r yet evolving. We r yet discovering things about ourselves. We are these shapely magnificent people called fe'melle in French. (See Women's intuition and refer back to Dana Dorfman as stated earlier) I think a woman's intuition is the greatest gift she was given by her creator. It's nothing like it and it scares the heck out of man. Back in the dark ages people consider it as tapering around with the dark art and women were hanged for that reason. She could not tell what she feels or see before it happens. After the dark ages it became "a gut feeling." The language changes and so do the words. Well this so call gut feeling could kick in while she's doing her daily chores, shopping, driving, socializing, at a doctor's office, relaxing and reading a book. It can happen any where at any time.

How does she know something is wrong with her child at school while she is at work? How does she know to call up a relative that she hasn't heard from in awhile? How does she know that someone in danger? How does she know if her husband's having an affair? How does she know when a person is lying? We were made born with it. Sometimes our signals can get crossed when someone is covering up a lie and you want to give him or her the benefit of the doubt.

Then, it becomes the matter of you going in the opposite direction and then later you find out that you have just avoided an accident and it could have been u.

Intuition is a warning a strong gut feeling that is built inside of us. Haven't you heard people say?

- "I had a feeling he was lying."
- "Something is wrong with my child, I better call the school."
- "My husband is having an affair?"
- "I have a feeling that my boyfriend has cheated on me, but I'm too afraid to ask him about it, because I know he'll only deny it."

HEAVENLY BODY: Our bodies go through a lot.

A man should study with caution and learn with caution. There is a little known fact if puberty doesn't shake her world menopause will. Puberty is a way of getting us prepared of what's to come when we start getting older. When a girl reaches puberty she gets a first period, fatigue, headaches, breast tenderness bloating and cramps that make her whole body ache. It feels like someone is shaping and bending our bodies into something that we don't know until we reach the age of maturity. I would like to use one of my favorite quotes from Charles Dickens to compare it, "It was the best of times, it was the worst of times, it was the age of enlightenment, it was the age of fooliness."

Although, it has many meanings, I don't think he had only a male in mind when he wrote this piece. No one writes like this anymore. You have to go to the classic if you really want to read good solid

well-written books. Movies and books r filled with sex, violence, porn, and profanity. Even the singers has no sense of decency...they want to take their clothes
off and get naked in front of a camera. The sound of their voice is covered with insecurity. They don't think they will sell a million albums if they don't get halfway naked.

If a man thinks he's the leader he's right, but give account. Behind every man...need I say more?
When someone belittles u, that person was also belittled and they have become their own worse enemy. Get Free! Get Help!

Women's blue print: I am fearfully and wonderfully made

We are so complex with all the things our bodies send us through we both better be glad somebody out there wants to put with us.

Women love to read things on improvement, magazine, and books. We love watching talk show about relationship as if the other woman never had to go through any thing. We want to know how she dealt with problems and stinky situations. Yes, I said, stinky, because after it becomes stinky, it stinks up the place.

We never stop to think that men don't have a care in the world, but they do. We can't keep seeing things one-sided. We have to learn to look at things as if though we have never seen it or heard it before. We have to view life with a fresh pair of eyes, like putting on new contacts of glasses 2 c clear enough. We have to approach things with a fresh thought in mind. Just maybe we might see the world like our creator sees it: Worth creating and worth saving!

What's on Ur list?

HERE'S 2 U MA'AM/ If you don't want to know don't ask

There's an elephant in the room and be careful what u ask for! Remember the guy who called me ma'am now here is the real deal about this word and where it originated from:

It arrived from England and all southern people get tied up in knots over this word because that's what they were taught. Yeah, and taught wrong! But, to keep kids in line as a respect tool by telling them they were disrespectful if they didn't say the word to an older person including an aunt, big sister, and cousin, etc., was wrong.

Eventually, materialistically poor Scotch Irish migrated to America and became owners of people, making them property. Of course, they gained respect among some and some were even hated because of their Irish blood, but still felt as important as the great mother England. This doesn't dismiss the fact that all people felt inferior at one time to another group of great importance. As for the usage of words visit your online dictionary or word search. Better yet, walk in a library and they will have plenty of answers for u.

The south doesn't own this word, but they made it a part of their cultural history. The west probably would argue that they were the first to use it as well. It is also commonly used out west. For most people like Natalie Angier who prefers not to be called ma'am...yeah...I think because we have used it for so long that for older women, it does tend to make u feel a lot older than what u r.

As long as my children show me respect the word isn't necessary and I'm speaking of course from the generation I can from. I'm not going to beat them because they don't call me ma'am. Believe me, I got plenty of whippings became I didn't say the word. I grew up in the south and it did make me feel bad. If we got into any trouble were to lower our head in shame and said, "Yes, ma'am". It reminded me of beatings and that I deserved to be beaten because of something I did or did not do.

Don't blame them because they usually think there ways r right. It did keep the kids in line didn't it? Really! The entire yes ma'am and no ma'am didn't make them better people. Tell it to the judge that sentences many of them to jail for disobeying the law. Now, to get back to its originality, *ma'am* is a derivation of madam applied to only women of upper classes or nobility. All the upper class English people along with their servants and from the poor on the streets of Jolly ol' England came by ship (the Mayflower) and landed on Plymouth Rock.

Say the word back to young people to make them feel old.

LOL

ABOUT THE AUTHOR

Izola Bird found her passion in writing at an early age. As an adult, she started as a freelance writer for various newspapers and magazines. She is a volunteer in her community and has won many awards. She is a member of Indiana Black Expo, South Bend Chapter and a former member of fourteen years with Women in Touch/Breast Cancer group. She is also a field Missionary and has worked with a homeless center, Hope Rescue and Christian Prison Fellowship. Izola Bird publishes a Christian newsletter annually entitled, 2-Soar.

Izola Bird is known throughout her community as a local writer. She worked as a Paraprofessional for ten years, now she has taken some time off to promote her books and plays.

IZOLA BIRD'S WRITING CREDITS

***

- Over two hundred published short stories and articles.
- Has interviewed four celebrities:
  a. **Spike Lee,** Chicago Defender March 5, 1991, An Evening With Spike Lee
  b. **Robb Armstrong - The Young Cartoonist**, Communicator July 6, 1991
  c. Publisher Clarence Nabba (retired)
  d. **Colin Powell**, Tri-State Defender July 25, 1992
  e. **Alice Walker -** Expression Newspaper at Ivy Tech College June 5, 1991, formerly senior editor Tracie Jacobs
- Two books published entitled, *The Sweet Grapes* in *New South Wales, Australia* available on e-books, (has earned five stars) and *Burning the Mattress* release date May 5, 2008 by Publish America. Her recent book entitled, *The Witch That Stole My Husband,* is available at the local library, Amazon.com and Barnes and Noble.com.

Plays

The Straw Women Who Made Bricks, performed at MLK Center June 27, 2009, St. Paul Memorial Methodist Church
June 12, 2009. The Straw Women Who Made Bricks at the Indiana Historical Center Indianapolis June 18, 20011
Ed's Revelation, a radio soap drama mystery 2008-09

Radio
Ed's Revelation aired on WUBS Radio Station 89.7FM
October 2008-2009.
The Straw Women Who Made Bricks WUBS 2011

Published Articles:
Many of Izola's collection of articles, short stories are
not shown here. Many of her earlier works as a free
lance writer were never recorded. There were over
two hundred published pieces that were written by
the author.

ACKNOWLEGEMENTS

Thanks to all of u and for some of u that didn't even realize I was watching and taking notes.

To friends and family - Connie Goldman of *Late Life Love,* Dr. Grey, Kevin Howard. Quotes from Charles Dickens, William Wordsworth and Meredith McGuire, William Wordsworth, Daniela Gioseffi 1997, *If a woman told the truth it would split the whole world open*, Muriel Rukeyse.

My own personal reviews of some movies old movie I've seen. Movie reviews, Queens of Kings, Braking all the Rules, The list, 7 things to do before I'm 30, Eat Pray Love, Hallmark Channel, Barbara Streisand, Sana Dorfman, A woman's intuition on line, Maya Angelou, Book of Solomon, Whitney Houston, Shakespear, The Gift Hitch, Dance With Me and thanks to Wikipedia on line, Olivia Newton John, Eddie Courtship, My Three sons, Andy Griffin, Different Strokes, which have been mentioned in the book.

Thanks to everyone who contributed to this book!
As always, thanks Pat Blackwell and Peggy who have always supported me!

Last, but certainly not least Edward Smith (The guru on young men's behavior when they are chasing girls) except for a few, and Cori Graham for his opinion about the girlfriend's list. Even, Jay Finley May a straight to the point kind of guy who always have something to say about men and women. Many other young men and young women I interviewed for this book. Thanks to the wonderful security at the South Bend Public Library and a special thank to the most kindness, Walter Morris who always has a smile on his face. Thanks to all of the staff at the South Bend Public Library!

Author's Note

Did you know that we have sixty thousand thoughts a day? "The right side of the brain is responsible for our imagination, dreams and subconscious thoughts. Our subconscious thoughts are our own dreams - Imagine that! Uhm...While most people use the left side of the brain more often focusing on logic and reasoning, those who utilize both sides have better memories and intellectual abilities. When a person has a stroke the left side is affected. Speech and actions cannot move forth.

When people are able to use both sides of the brain equally, they are called geniuses, but when they are able to skillfully use only half, they are called talented. Great thinkers come intelligently inclined. The lazy minds are confused. They don't know which way is up. Dreamers are stuck in mid-air. They are just dreaming about what they can do, but don't have the intelligent to make it happen. This book is filled with wonderful sayings and mentions classic books and idioms. It will make u laugh about some of the subject matter. I talk about celebrities as well as I discuss the movies they were in. I have also quoted some very famous authors such as Dr. Grey of *Men Are from Mars and Women Are from Venus*.

Meredith McGuire says, "The truth can perform a series of permutations, creating multiple versions of it, each equally accurate and equally flawed. The truth is capable of taking on a life of its own." In other words, we see what we want to see. We would rather eat the trash out of the garbage rather than really see those flaws. Think about it!

-Izola

CONTACT INFORMATION

Izola loves to hear from her readers. To request additional copies of this book or to invite the author to speak at your event, contact her at:

Email: thestrawwomen@gmail.com

Izola Bird

DORINU PUBLICATIONS
© 04/2012

www.ingramcontent.com/pod-product-compliance
Lightning Source LLC
Chambersburg PA
CBHW052205270326
41931CB00011B/2234